Chalking It Up To Experience:
Second Edition

Authors:

Perry A. Castelli, Ph.D

Vivian L. Castelli, M. Ed.

Sheepdog Publishing of Lakeland
P. O. Box 625
Highland City, Florida 33846
Sheepdogpub@aol.com

http://www.esmartweb.sheepdogpub.com

ISBN: 0-9714972-0-6

Printing by InstantPublisher.com

Chalking It Up To Experience

Acknowledgements

Indirectly speaking, literally thousands of students have helped to shape this book over the past thirty years. Ranging in ages from three to eighty-three, our students have provided us with a repertoire of "best practices' that transformed our teaching careers from a job to a joy! Within this text we have attempted to capture and annotate select examples of successful strategies in an effort to assist new and experienced teachers in their daily performance. Consequently, it becomes incumbent upon us to acknowledge and to thank all of our former students who through one avenue or another have contributed to the creation of this text.

It is our pleasure to personally thank the following teachers and administrators who took their valuable time to read and review earlier versions of the text. Through their efforts, they have collectively breathed new life into the ideas and afforded additional authenticity to the original thoughts. We are grateful for the improvements and enhancements that they brought to the text. They are:

Scott Bozeman
Middle School Music Teacher
Savannah, GA

Jon Burnett
Drama Teacher, Actor
San Francisco, CA

Rebecca Castelli
Vocal Instructor, Actress
San Francisco, CA

Jackie Ennis
Middle School Teacher
College Professor
Barton College, Wilson, NC

Lori Allen
Nationally Board Certified Teacher
Human Resource Development
Polk County School System, Florida

Suzanne Houff
College Professor
Mary Washington College, VA

James Kimbrough
President of SACS
Former Dean, School of Education
Troy State University, AL

Paula Leftwich
Director of Teacher Education
Florida Southern College

Margaret Lucas
High School Librarian/Media Specialist
Euclid, Ohio

Douglas MacIsaac
College Professor
Florida Southern College, Orlando

Barbara Marshall
High School Mathematics
Canton, MI

Terri Mathews
High School Music Teacher
Bel Air, MD

Barbara Mize
College Professor
Barton College, Wilson, NC

Yvonne Morrow
College Professor
Warner Southern College, FL

Sally S. Naylor
Dean, College of Education
St. Petersburg College, FL

Darrell Pearson
College Professor
Troy State University, AL

Pia Restina
Middle School Art Teacher
Polk County School System, FL

Judy Senzamici
College Professor
Florida Southern College, FL

Sheron White
Elementary School Music Teacher
Lakeland, FL

Additionally, we would like to express our gratitude to the following junior and senior education majors from Florida Southern College in Lakeland, Florida. These students utilized an early copy of the text in their student teaching seminar. They have provided us with a detailed written review on the merit and worthiness of the text. They are:

Melissa Freeman-Gray
Michelle Hearndon
Rachel M. Jandeska
Kristin LaMonda
Jessica Lanier
Kristi L. Mills

Brittani Opalinski
Dana Parrish
Jennifer Sanders
Nicole Sawicki
Elizabeth Wagner

Finally, we would like to take this opportunity to extend our deepest gratitude to Mrs. Anna Maria DiCesare. Mrs. DiCesare is a former teacher and administrator in the Polk County School System in Bartow, Florida. Currently, Mrs. DiCesare is the Coordinator of Field Experiences at Florida Southern College in Lakeland, Florida. In this capacity she oversees numerous interns each year, working with them "out in the field," and then facilitating the student teaching seminar for the "new" teachers back on campus. Mrs. DiCesare adopted an early copy of the text for use in her student teaching seminar. The students listed previously were members of her class. Mrs. DiCesare personally spent numerous hours reading and reviewing the text, as well as, employing the book in her class-room. We are grateful!

Chalking It Up To Experience

Foreword

The publication of this book continues to focus on the beginning teacher and all the guidelines needed to give confidence in all the aspects of teaching.

I continue to appreciate the work done by the two authors. Their many years in the profession are shown in the current information used in the book. It is timely, accurate and positive... If this book is used as a resource often and correctly, the reader can receive lots of practical knowledge needed to be a diligent educator.

The format of the book is improved and very precise for the reader. It brings together many meaningful experiences, useful resources and lots of suggestions.

.

by Anna Maria DiCesare,
Coordinator of Field Experiences
Education Department
Florida Southern College

Chalking It Up To Experience

Table of Contents

Acknowledgements v

Foreword x

Table of Contents... xiii

Preface xv

Introduction xvii

Chapter   1   Acquiring a Teaching Position 1

Chapter   2   Starting the Year Off Right 17

Chapter   3   Evaluation / Assessment.................................... 33

Chapter   4   Understanding Students and Your Subject......... 49

Chapter   5   Motivation and Critical Thinking...................... 65

Chapter   6   Classroom Management 83

Chapter   7   Dealing With Stress... 100

Chapter   8   Know the Essentials of School Law 116

Chapter   9   Working With Parents and Administrators....... 137

Chapter   10   Utilizing Technology....................................... 154

Chapter   11   Meeting the Needs of Diverse Students 173

Chapter   12   Professionalism... 189

Appendices 209

Biographical Information 218

Index 220

Alignment to Florida Educator Accomplished Practices 224

Chalking It Up To Experience

Preface

This second addition of **"Chalking It Up To Experience"** has instituted a number of changes based on the work of preservice and inservice teachers, college and university faculty, and the literacy/research base of learned societies in education and psychology. Two new chapters have been added (**<u>Evaluation and Assessment</u>** and **<u>Understanding Students and Your Subject</u>**) and all chapters have been updated and revised (including expanded resources) to meet the needs of tomorrow's classrooms.

This book is designed intentionally to be very concise, brief, and a jumping off point for preservice teachers, new teachers, and inservice teachers. There are no in-depth topics because we wanted both new and experienced teachers to have a tool that is arranged simply and **provides important information quickly at those times when swift, but well thought out and well practiced ideas are needed.** In addition, there are a **variety of resources** in each chapter (**books, journals,** and **web sites**) provided for those times that the teacher may want to research a topic in more detail.

We have been teaching a combined total of over 50 years and have developed certain standards that have helped us in our teaching. We have both taught elementary, middle and high school students as well as undergraduate and graduate students in colleges. We have taught in inner cities, suburbs, and rural communities. We have taught young people of diverse ethnic, racial and socioeconomic backgrounds successfully. We have helped to develop curriculum and been integral in the implementation of technology in schools. Therefore, we hope that some of **our experience gleaned over our many years of teaching will help others who are thinking about teaching, about to teach, teaching their first year, or who have taught for a while, but need some suggestions from time to time.**

Chalking It Up To Experience

Introduction

This book is now arranged into twelve chapters that we believe are imperative to success in teaching. **The primary ingredient for success in teaching is, of course, a love of teaching and the young people that you teach**. But it is not enough sometimes when the road gets rough and the adventure gets rocky. That is why we have put together suggestions from our personal experiences and relevant research in an organized manner so that ideas can be easily located inside the pages of this book. When looking for that first teaching position or planning an upcoming conference with parents, we believe that this book can be of use to preservice and new inservice teachers on almost a daily basis. **We share a love of teaching with all of you and want to help to make your teaching career one of continual delight and success.** So please refer to our book frequently and we salute you for entering the best profession in the world - TEACHING!

"It is the obligation of the teacher,
to make the agony of decision making so intense,
that the only escape is by thinking!"
~~*Perry & Vivian Castelli*
<u>**Social Foundations of American Education**</u>
2nd edition   (2000)   Carolina Academic Press

xvii

Chalking It Up To Experience

Chapter 1: Acquiring a Teaching Position

RIGHT **NOW** is an excellent time to be looking for a teaching position! Salaries, benefits, and support systems have never been better. **A nationwide teacher shortage** has gripped the United States for the past five years and will continue well beyond the first decade of the twenty-first century. Elementary and secondary school student enrollments are on the rise and a record number of teachers (baby boomers) are reaching retirement age. Positions are available in all teaching fields and located in areas ranging from inner city schools to suburban and rural districts. Two key factors which will assist new teachers to find and secure employment are: (1) **the ability to relocate to "where" the position is**, and (2) **the competency to professionally present oneself first on paper (cover letter, resume, etc.), and then in person** (interview). This chapter outlines strategies designed to acquaint oneself with the culture of a school; steps necessary to prepare for a job search; preparing for and successfully navigating an interview (especially how to handle the all-important question -- *What is your philosophy of education?);* and steps to take after an interview concludes and you have returned home! The overriding principle in effect that guides the importance of this first chapter is preparation … remember, **failure to plan is planning for failure!**

I. Preparation

- 📖 Begin **volunteering** wherever there are opportunities to work with young children or teens, such as church, YMCA, daycares, summer camps, etc.

- 📖 Be a **good student** in college to give you the right background of knowledge to teach.

- 📖 Take any **required teacher tests** as early as possible so that any retests can be done with less pressure.

- 📖 If you encounter problems on any of the **required teacher tests**, seek **help immediately** in the form of **tutoring** or **classes** to prepare for the tests.

- 📖 Build a **rapport** with the **community** by participating in community activities to be visible and maintain a good reputation.

- 📖 Begin accumulating idea **books** and **teaching materials** that may be useful to you in your teaching.

- 📖 Volunteer to work with **different age levels** to best determine the age group with which you would like to work.

- 📖 **Learn skills** such as computer, crafts, etc. that will be beneficial to you when you teach.

- 📖 Build a **support network** as you volunteer, attend college, student teach, etc. that you may use for references, etc.

- 📖 Exercise and eat right to build **strength** and **stamina**.

Networking has been determined as a very important task for anyone in any profession. Seek the support of those who know your capabilities. Always be gracious and thank those who give you support and assistance as you begin your career!

II.   Get Organized

☐ **After you graduate secure a copy of your transcript** and check that everything is posted correctly.

☐ Obtain permission from those you **plan to use as references.**

☐ **Acquire letters of recommendation** from those who are knowledgeable of your work in the classroom.

☐ **Prepare a portfolio** to take with you to interviews (see section IV of this chapter).

☐ Prepare a **resume** that is **professional** and **concise**. Be sure to **review** it **yearly**. (See the section on preparing a resume in this chapter.)

☐ Formulate or locate a list of **possible interview questions.** (See Appendix I: Ten Most Difficult Interview Questions)

☐ **Practice answering the possible interview questions**; write out answers; tape record your responses; and/or rehearse with another person listening to your replies.

☐ **Prepare a list of questions that you will want to ask**. These should be centered on the professional aspects of the position (e.g. methodology, technology, facilities, equipment, supplies, etc.) In your initial interview, avoid the salary and benefit topic unless you need an immediate answer.

☐ **Find out as much as possible about the school systems** with which you want to apply and eventually interview.

☐ **Learn the names and positions of essential personnel** in the school systems you wish to apply and interview.

III. The Resume

- 📖 **Your name should appear in larger text** at the top of the page.

- 📖 **Education and experience should be listed in order of the most recent** to that of prior years.

- 📖 **List institutions and degrees before dates** to emphasize those factors.

- 📖 **Include Technology Experience** that emphasizes applications you can easily utilize and various educational software programs with which you are familiar.

- 📖 **List volunteer experience** in addition to work experience whenever pertinent.

- 📖 **List references' names, addresses, telephone and email.**

- 📖 **Emphasize the positive and avoid the negative**, but always be honest.

- 📖 Be sure that all information is **easily read and that the resume is neat.**

- 📖 **Proofread and ask others to proofread** the resume for any typographical errors, etc.

- 📖 Try to **limit the resume to one page** if at all possible.

A good resume will only get you an interview. What determines your success in obtaining a job is bringing the resume to life, showing that you are whom you say you are! While preparing the resume, determine ways that you can show your assets!

IV. Portfolios

- Include a **resume and a written philosophy of teaching.** (See the sections on preparing a resume and writing a philosophy in this chapter.)
- **Provide detailed lesson plans** that you have actually used.
- Display your prowess at the **computer through spreadsheet gradebooks, learning databases, letters to parents,** etc.
- Furnish **field experience** and **student teaching evaluations** as well as letters of commendation.
- **Include any letters you may have received from volunteer work,** student teaching, etc. that praise your teaching abilities.
- **Exhibit any publications you have written** or that were written about something you participated in and mention you by name.
- **Take pictures of bulletin boards, you and your students, etc.** during student teaching, volunteer work, etc. to place in the portfolio.
- Place a **copy of your transcript** in the portfolio.
- **Display examples or pictures of any talent** you may have such as crafts, sewing, artwork, etc.
- **Prepare a video of yourself teaching** a successful lesson.

Hopefully you have planned ahead and have accumulated the above mentioned items over your college years and possibly before. Preparation cannot be under rated.

V.   Develop a Philosophy of Teaching

- 📖 Examine **historical educational philosophies** to establish whether you personify any of the particular philosophies.

- 📖 Be able to answer the question, **"Why do I want to teach?"**

- 📖 Know what your **beliefs** are about what comprises good **teaching**.

- 📖 Establish **why** you have chosen the **particular subject** or **grade level** that you wish to teach.

- 📖 Think about the **teachers** who have been your **role models** and **what special qualities you admire** and plan to **emulate**.

- 📖 Decide what **classroom management** style or what elements will make up your classroom management.

- 📖 Determine your **beliefs** about students, how they learn and individual capabilities. How will you use this to improve your teaching?

- 📖 **Ascertain your teaching style** and whether all students will benefit from it and how will you motivate students to learn in your classroom.

- 📖 Declare **expectations** you will have of **yourself** as a teacher and what **expectations** you will have of **your students**.

- 📖 **Write** out your philosophy of teaching and **continually review** and **alter** it as necessary.

Be wise! Know exactly WHY you want to teach!

VI.   Investigate

- 📖 **Write or call to obtain information** about the school districts in which you are interested.

- 📖 **Use the Internet to obtain information** about the school districts in which you are interested.

- 📖 **Utilize the Chamber of Commerce** to learn more about the community.

- 📖 Organize a **list of questions** to explore concerning the community and its relationship to the schools.

- 📖 **Obtain local newspapers** from the community that may give you information on activities, funding, etc. in the school district.

- 📖 **Attend events in the community** to get a feel for the **community.**

- 📖 **Talk to teachers** you may meet in the community or arrange to **interview** a teacher.

- 📖 **Volunteer in the community** or in **schools** nearby during your college preparation.

- 📖 Be able to answer the question convincingly, **"How will I fit into this school and the community?"**

- 📖 Be able to **discuss your knowledge** you have gained about the school district and the community.

You can be assured that the community members will want to know about you, so be sure to likewise show interest by knowing all you can about the community in which you want to teach!

VII. Applications

- 📖 Call or visit to **secure applications from the school districts** to which you wish to apply in a timely manner.

- 📖 **Make a work copy of the application** on which to compile the necessary information before actually doing the finished copy.

- 📖 Pay close attention to the specifics or **details that are asked and questions that** you are expected to answer, and answer them directly.

- 📖 Be **truthful** completing the **application.** Reveal any **problems** with the **law.**

- 📖 **Type or print all information** so that it is easily read, unless otherwise directed.

- 📖 **Be sure to include all requested information and documents** or request transcripts, letters of reference, etc. as necessary and immediately.

- 📖 Keep **tobacco, food, drink, makeup, etc. away** from the **application** so that the application is neat and clean.

- 📖 Compose a **short cover letter** that **expresses your interest in a teaching** position and accentuates some of your excellent teaching qualifications.

- 📖 If requested to have reference letters sent directly to the school district, **follow up with a phone call in about ten days to check on the status of your application** primarily to determine if they have received your reference letters, transcripts, etc.

- 📖 **Politely call personnel and request information regarding teaching positions** with the school district to underscore your interest in the positions.

VIII. Appearance for the Interview

- Invest in proper attire that makes you look and feel professional for an interview. Navy blue and other dark colors are considered interview colors.

- It is better to be overdressed for the interview than to be underdressed.

- Wear subdued colognes for interviews.

- Women should wear subtle makeup for interviews.

- Keep all jewelry simple and modest.

- Although body piercing is the style, it would be best to leave the piercing jewelry at home.

- Procure the opinion of someone you trust concerning your interview attire.

- Wear comfortable and sensible shoes to an interview.

- Be sure to bathe and use a deodorant to avoid any negative body odor.

- Be conscious of good posture, it makes you look more assertive.

- Lean toward a conservative look.

You will not get a <u>second</u> chance to make a <u>first</u> impression.

What the future employer sees

at an interview will leave

a *lasting* impression!

IX. The Interview

- 📖 **Be prompt and arrive alone.**

- 📖 **Be prepared for any variety of interviews:** one-to-one, two-to-one, group interviewees answering questions, audiotaped or videotaped, etc.

- 📖 **Keep good eye contact** with the interviewer(s) and use good **listening skills**.

- 📖 Offer a **firm handshake** to establish that you are **confident,**

- 📖 **Always remain positive,** even when asked to tell about a weakness. ("I tend to put a lot of pressure on myself to do as much as humanly possible.") **Turn weaknesses into strengths**!

- 📖 **Be assertive and emphasize** your accomplishments.

- 📖 **Always be honest** and answer all questions directly. Unfortunately, you may be asked illegal questions you should not answer. However, if you protest, you probably won't get the job.

- 📖 **Discuss activities, accomplishments, your philosophy, and goals** to establish your positive attributes.

- 📖 **Present your portfolio** to help emphasize your positive attributes and accomplishments.

- 📖 **Ask questions** to demonstrate that you have researched the school district and that you are actively interested in the teaching position.

Don't be modest!

Get to the point!

Be honest and sincere!

X.   Follow Up to the Interview

📖 End the interview on the same positive note that it began: with a **firm handshake, good eye contact, and a verbal goodbye.**

📖 **Emphasize your appreciation, your interest** in the position, and **your desire** to **hear** from the interviewer(s).

📖 **Send a thank you note to the interviewer(s)** when you get home to help accentuate your positive attributes and to re-establish your name for the interviewer(s).

📖 **Utilize a follow up phone call** to check on the status of your application and interview.

📖 Continue to **evaluate and consider how you can improve your interviews.**

📖 **Resume practice interviewing with someone.** Have them give you questions to answer that you may encounter at some time in an interview.

📖 **Persevere to apply and to interview**, as practice will make you a better interviewee.

📖 Contemplate working as an **aide or a substitute** if nothing comes of your applications and interviews, because this may lead to a teaching position.

📖 Consider moving to an **area that has a higher demand** for new teachers if the market is not good where you live.

📖 **Persist in working for an advanced degree** in education to make yourself more marketable.

<u>Notes</u>

<u>Notes</u>

References and Resources

Books:

📖 Adams Bullock, Ann and Parmalee Hawk, *Developing a Teaching Portfolio: A Guide for Preservice and Practicing Teachers*. Upper saddle River, NJ: Prentice Hall, Inc., 2001

📖 Calhoun, Florence, *Choosing a Career in Teaching*. New York: Rosen Publishing Group, 2000.

📖 Campbell, Dorothy M., *How to Develop a Professional Portfolio: A Manual for Teachers*. Needham Heights, MA: Allyn and Bacon, 1997.

📖 Costantino, Patricia M., *Developing a Professional Teaching Portfolio: A Guide for Success*. Boston, MA: Allyn and Bacon, 2002.

📖 Cutlip, Glen W., *Careers in Teaching*. New York: The Rosen Publishing Group, 1997.

📖 Dougherty, Anne, *Beginnings: A Guide for New Teachers.* Coronada, CA: A. Dougherty Publisher, 1988.

📖 Freire, Paulo, *Teachers As Cultural Workers: Letters To Those Who Dare Teach.* Boulder, CO: Westview Press, 1998

📖 Meyer, Jan, *Career Opportunities As A Computer Instructor*. Chicago: Institute for Research, 1999.

📖 *Opportunities As A Teacher, High School Math and Science*. Chicago: Institute for Research, 1998.

📖 Parkay, Forrest W., *Becoming A Teacher*. Boston: Allyn and Bacon, 1998.

📖 *Resumes for Education Careers*. Lincolnwood, IL: VGM Career Horizons, 1999.

📖 Sarason, Seymour Bernard, *You Are Thinking of Teaching?: Opportunities, Problems, Realities*. San Francisco: Jossey-Bass, 1993.

📖 Schomp, Virginia, *If You Were a - Teacher*. Tarrytown, NY: Benchmark books, 1999.

📖 Seldin, Peter, *How To Produce A Teaching Portfolio, 2nd ed.*, Boston: Anker Publishing Co, 2000

📖 Seldin, Peter, *The Teaching Portfolio: A Practical Guide to Improved Performance and Promotion.* Boston: Anker Publishing Co., 1997.

Journals and Magazines:

📖 **Directory of Public Schools in the US:** American Association for Employment in Education; 820 Davis St, Ste 222, Evanston, IL 60201-4445; **E-mail**: aaee@nwu.edu; Phone: 847-864-1999.

📖 **Education Standard:** M I I Publications, 733 15th St NW Ste 900, Washington, DC 20005-2112; Phone 202-347-4822.

📖 **Guide to Summer Camps and Summer Schools:** Porter Sargent Publishers, 11 Beacon St. Ste 1400, Boston, MA 02108; E-mail: info@portersargent.com, Phone: 617-523-1670.

📖 **Handbook of Private Schools:** Porter Sargent Publishers, 11 Beacon St. Ste 1400, Boston, MA 02108, E-mail: info@portersargent.com; Phone 617-523-1670.

📖 **New Teacher Advocate:** Kappa Delta Pi, 3707 Woodview Trace, PO box 2669, Indianapolis IN 46268-1158; Phone: 317-871-4900

📖 **Next Step Magazine;** PO Box 405, Victor, NY 14564-0405; E-mail: feedback@nextstepmag.com; Phone: 716-742-1260

📖 **Patterson's American Education:** Educational Directories Inc.; PO Box 199, Mount Prospect, IL 60056-0199; Phone: 847-459-0605

📖 **Theory into Practice:** Ohio State University, 172 Arps Hall, 1945 N. High St., Columbus, OH 43210-1172; E-mail: tip@osu.edu; Phone: 614-292-3407.

📖 More online at **http://www.publist.com**

Internet Sites:

📖 **Academic Employment Network,** http://www.academploy.com/, teaching and administrative jobs

📖 **ACADEMIC EMPLOYMENT NETWORK:** http://www.academploy.com/, jobs for K-12 teachers.

📖 **Career Builder**, Search: teacher, www.CareerBuilder.com

📖 **Education Job Openings:** http://www.nationjob.com/education.

📖 **EDUCATION JOBS:** http://www.nationjob.com/(Search: education), lists jobs specifically related to teaching

📖 **EDUCATION OPENINGS:** helps to locate teaching positions. http://www.educationopenings.com/,

📖 **K-12 Jobs.com:** http://www.k12jobs.com/, kindergarten through vocational teaching positions.

📖 **Resources for Indispensable Schools and Educators, http://www.risenetwork.org/teachers.html**.

📖 **Teacher Hiring**, Best practices for hiring teachers. www.**teacherhiring**.net

📖 **Teacher Jobs**: http://www.teacherjobs.com, searchable resume and job postings.

📖 **TEACHERS.NET**: http://jobs.teachers.net/data/jobcenter/. Resource for finding K-12 positions, etc.

📖 **Teachersplanet.com** – Select *Teaching Jobs*. http:teachersplanet.com

📖 **Teachers-Teachers.com:** http://www.teachers-teachers.com/, free service

Chapter 2: Starting the Year Off Right

All teachers, whether first year teachers or veteran teachers, need to start the year off right. It sets the basis for the entire year and is worth the necessary planning. **One of the key ingredients to being a good teacher is preparation**. It is never too soon to begin getting ready for the following year. Planning should be an on going process as teachers analyze, synthesize, review, and evaluate their teaching throughout the year. Prepared teachers discard unsuccessful plans and lessons when they are not working, and only keep those that are effective. Successful teachers are constantly thinking about how to improve and expand upon what is already being done.

However, the culmination of all of the planning evolves during the last weeks prior to the beginning of school when **detailed planning** is necessary to get the year rolling. This is a very important time and what a teacher does with this time can make or break the school year. **It is never good to be behind in planning and trying to catch up, because most teachers would agree, catching up never happens.** Therefore, experienced teachers try to avoid the last minute, night before school starts preparation. It is too stressful and may often lead to a school year of frustration. One of the disadvantages of being a first year teacher is that generally they cannot pull from a background of experience. Successful, well-planned, veteran teachers know what and how to get the school year off to a good beginning (so consider them an important resource). There are many vital things that can be done before the start of school to make life easier for the teacher. Accumulated in this chapter are just a few suggestions of things teachers can do to get the school year off to a good start.

**Starting the
school year
well prepared
is one of the
best guarantees
for a good**

I. Move At Least Two Weeks Before School Starts

- 📖 Make a **moving checklist** and cross things off as they are accomplished.

- 📖 Unload personal teaching materials **AT THE SCHOOL**, not at your new home.

- 📖 Check the **Chamber of Commerce** and the **School Board** to find out about the area.

- 📖 Find the **shortest and safest route** to school.

- 📖 Find **alternate routes** to school.

- 📖 Make a **trial run** at the time you will travel to school **before** the first day.

- 📖 Locate public libraries, museums, and all possible **teaching resources**.

- 📖 **Familiarize** yourself with **driving** and **walking** in the area well before school starts.

- 📖 Make acquaintances with your new neighbors **BEFORE** school starts.

- 📖 **Relax** and take some time to enjoy your new environment and do something totally unrelated to school.

PREPARATION: groundwork, organization, readiness, adaptation, grooming, readying, putting in order, training, anticipation, rehearsal, arrangement, tuning, foundation, preliminaries, forecast, equip, facilitate, measure, cultivation, elaboration, sharpening, mature, practice, mellow!

II.   Get Into School Prior To Mandatory Dates

- 📖 Check with the **office** to see if there are any changes that you should be aware of for the coming school year.
- 📖 Put up **bulletin boards**.
- 📖 **Clean** and **dust** the classroom.
- 📖 While dressed comfortably, take materials gathered during the summer into school **prior to mandatory days**.
- 📖 Return any **borrowed equipment** such as computers before school starts.
- 📖 Take advantage of this time to **meet new staff**.
- 📖 Retrieve and/or check **multimedia equipment functioning**.
- 📖 Gather paper, paste, pens, pencils, etc. from **supply room**.
- 📖 Check to find out what **new equipment** and **media** has been acquired for teacher use.
- 📖 Accrue **schedules**, **rosters**, and any other **important information** with which to begin familiarizing yourself.

"Good Teaching is one-fourth preparation and three-fourths theatre."

- Gail Godwin

Englewood Cliffs, New Jersey: Prentice Hall, 1992, p.84

III. Seek Safe and Reliable Volunteers to Help

- First check **local and state guidelines**. Many states now require **extensive screening** of **ALL volunteers** for the **protection** of **students**.

- Utilize the help of **family** to get your classroom prepared.

- Solicit help from **prior students** or their parents/guardians.

- Invite good friends or neighbors with **talents** to **share** into your classroom.

- Consider forming a club or group that includes **reliable upper grade students** in your school or system willing to help teachers with bulletin boards, organizing, activities, etc. (but **never** grading). Check the local high schools for future teachers organizations.

- Seek the assistance of **senior citizens** that might **benefit** from helping in your classroom.

- Work with a **colleague** to prepare your classrooms together.

- Set dates for the school year with **community personnel** in appropriate fields to come into your classroom as guest speakers.

- Locate **college students** in education (or possibly in other fields such as counseling or social services) who need experiences in the classroom.

- Set up **times** and **places** for each volunteer to be sure that you both are there.

- **Reward helpers** with favors of your own, cooked or baked items, teaching materials, snacks, etc.

IV. Plan and Organize

- Have **long range goals** and **short range** goals with **approximate dates** to accomplish these goals.

- Develop **objectives** and then plan how to reach them.

- Provide a bulletin board or part of the chalkboard to **share objectives** with your students and their parents/guardians.

- Have your plan book ready **every Friday afternoon.**

- Refer often to your **teacher handbook. Develop** your own handbook if your school does not provide one. (This should include, but is not limited to, copies of various **school forms** so that you know what data the forms require and, if permissible, you can **duplicate** and use them when needed. The school secretary can be very helpful in organizing such a manual.)

- Organize, "a place for everything, and everything in its place."

- Teach your **students** from the beginning always to **put things back** in their place after they use classroom materials

- **Handle mail only once.** Have a place for "mail you need to act upon" such as a file folder or a desk bin labeled "in" and "out."

- **Discard** mail that you have no use for in the circular file.

- Have a place for "**mail you need to reference**." A three ring binder can be good for such purposes or a file labeled as such in a file drawer.

- Be **<u>FLEXIBLE</u>** because no matter how well you plan you may have to change those plans.

V.　　Prepare Record Keeping

- ☐ Take a sheet of loose leaf or graph paper to make a **temporary roster** on which to do attendance the first days of school.

- ☐ When you are sure that your roster is going to remain relatively **stable**, put them into the **permanent** attendance book.

- ☐ Make a **spreadsheet** on the computer, to use as a **roster** for **attendance**.

- ☐ **Duplicate** the above **spreadsheet** and set it up for **recording grades**.

- ☐ Create a **database** on the computer for all your students that includes such **information** as parent/guardian names, addresses, date of birth, ages, telephone numbers, parent/guardians work telephone numbers, particular allergies or illnesses, etc.

- ☐ Make **backup disks** of any important records such as attendance or grades in the event of lost data.

- ☐ Make **seating charts** ahead of time and even place name cards on desks to help younger children find their seats.

- ☐ Have **alternative seating charts** ready for possible times when it seems necessary to change seats for the benefit of the teacher and the students.

Handwritten or computer

generated, be prepared

to keep records when

school starts!

VI. Eating, Sleeping and Exercise

- 📖 **Walking** is an excellent form of exercise that doesn't require a lot of effort. Walk with a significant other, a colleague, or a friend.

- 📖 **Walk** during **planning** periods at school or **before** or **after** school.

- 📖 Walk on a **treadmill** in **inclement weather** to stay consistent with your exercise routine.

- 📖 Organize an **after school wellness program** to meet perhaps two or three times a week after school to do low-impact aerobics, play basketball, play volleyball, or walk as a group. The school's physical education teacher may be an excellent resource person for such a program as well as the school nurse.

- 📖 **Individual sports** such as golf or **team sports** such as basketball may be the means to get regular exercise outside of the school arena

- 📖 **Fitness clubs** are more expensive, but for some they may provide the **equipment** and **motivation** to get them exercising.

- 📖 **Do not skip meals**, especially **breakfast**. Break the fast (breakfast) and **refuel** for the day's work.

- 📖 Eat a **balanced diet** from all the food groups to help you maintain your stamina. Do not abuse alcohol or drugs.

- 📖 **Avoid fad diets** that will sap your strength and perhaps your disposition. Keep a **bottle of water** and a **high protein bar** in your room for those times you can't get a good meal or have to skip lunch.

- 📖 Be sure to get **adequate sleep** to feel rejuvenated in the morning.

VII. Teach and Enforce Rules and Routines Immediately

📖 Review **school rules** with the students and discuss **why rules are necessary**.

📖 The very first day of school you should create **rules** with the **help of** your **students** to **empower** them to have a say in their classroom and how it will be governed (ownership).

📖 Make **rules** that are **positive statements** that tell students what to do that is right instead of emphasizing what **NOT** to do.

📖 Have consequences and begin to **enforce** the **rules** the class has developed **immediately**.

📖 Make **consequences reasonable** so that they can be enforced. Unreasonable consequences will offend students, administrators, and parents/guardians.

📖 Make certain that students **begin** to **follow rules** on the very **first day** and be **consistent**.

📖 **Review** the **rules** from time to time, especially if students seem to be forgetting or when new students arrive.

📖 **Empower** your students by allowing them to help **maintain** the **classroom** by having weekly or monthly assignments of **helpers** in the **classroom**.

📖 **Establish routines** for pencil sharpening, lunch signup, attendance taking, lining up, etc. the very **first day** and be **consistent**.

📖 **Model** the **rules** for the students.

VIII. Communicate Expectations to Parents/Guardians

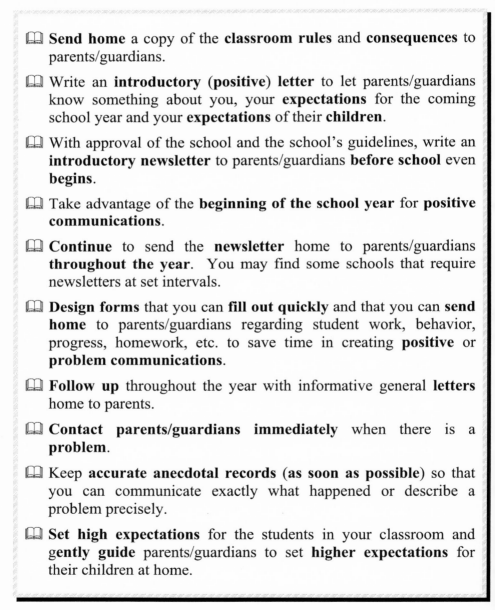

📖 **Send home** a copy of the **classroom rules** and **consequences** to parents/guardians.

📖 Write an **introductory (positive) letter** to let parents/guardians know something about you, your **expectations** for the coming school year and your **expectations** of their **children**.

📖 With approval of the school and the school's guidelines, write an **introductory newsletter** to parents/guardians **before school** even **begins**.

📖 Take advantage of the **beginning of the school year** for **positive communications**.

📖 **Continue** to send the **newsletter** home to parents/guardians **throughout the year**. You may find some schools that require newsletters at set intervals.

📖 **Design forms** that you can **fill out quickly** and that you can **send home** to parents/guardians regarding student work, behavior, progress, homework, etc. to save time in creating **positive** or **problem communications**.

📖 **Follow up** throughout the year with informative general **letters** home to parents.

📖 **Contact parents/guardians immediately** when there is a **problem**.

📖 Keep **accurate anecdotal records (as soon as possible)** so that you can communicate exactly what happened or describe a problem precisely.

📖 **Set high expectations** for the students in your classroom and **gently guide** parents/guardians to set **higher expectations** for their children at home.

IX.   Utilize Summer /Down Times To Gather Resources

📖 Seek resources that **compliment** the **curriculum**. Always be on the look out for **free materials** or **inexpensive books, posters,** etc.

📖 Investigate community organizations and businesses to find **people** to use as resources who are **experts** concerning parts of the **curriculum**.

📖 Take **photos** of people, places, animals, etc. when you travel that might enhance your instruction

📖 Visit **places** that you teach about and do first hand **tours**. Write down any **information** you learn during the tour that may add interest to the unit.

📖 Visit local **museums, government offices,** etc. to gather material or **information** for a unit.

📖 Go to **workshops** that are useful and of interest to you.

📖 Gather materials and shop around for materials that **compliment** your teaching units and that are **bargains** for a teacher's salary.

📖 A **rainy day** or one that is just **too hot** to go outside is a good time to go through **files** and discard or **reorganize files**.

📖 Take advantage of summer to take a **course** to work on your **professional hours (CEU's)**.

📖 **Learn something new** such as how to do a particular kind of art project or how to use a new software program, etc. that you can perhaps **share with** your **students**.

X.   Expect the Unexpected

- 📖 **Curriculum** may be rewritten. **Adjust** accordingly.

- 📖 **Schedules** may be varied. Be **FLEXIBLE**.

- 📖 **Personnel** may be changed. Look for ways to **help them**.

- 📖 The **grade level** one teaches may be exchanged. You become more **valuable**!

- 📖 The **subjects taught** may be modified with **additions** or **deletions**. Hopefully the **latter**.

- 📖 **Room assignments** may be shifted. **Get help** and **move**.

- 📖 **Textbooks** may be replaced. Dig into that **teacher's manual**!

- 📖 **Student classroom assignments** may be altered. Use a **temporary roster at first.**

- 📖 Have good **alternate lesson plans** with **interesting activities** ready for a **substitute**.

- 📖 **Model** for students **flexibility** and **acceptance** of **changes**.

28

<u>Notes</u>

<u>Notes</u>

References and Resources

Books:

📖 *Back-to-School Activities*. Teacher Created Materials Inc., June 1997.

📖 Blase, Joseph R., *The Fire is Back: Principals Sharing School Governance*. Corwin Press, Inc., September, 1996.

📖 Evans, Thomas W., *Mentors: Making a Difference in Our Public Schools*. Princeton, NJ: Peterson's Guides, 1992.

📖 Hall, Katy and Stephen Carpenter, *Back-to-School Belly Busters : And Other Side-Splitting Knock-Knock Jokes That Are Too Cool for School!* Harper Festival, 2002.

📖 Israel, Bess, *Best Ever Back to School Activities*. New York: Scholastic Publishing, 2001.

📖 *Mentoring, Developing Successful New Teachers*. Reston, VA: Association of Teacher E

📖 Odell, Sandra J., *Mentor Teacher Programs*. Washington D.C.: NEA Professional Library, 1990.

📖 Podsen, India, *Coaching and Mentoring First-Year and Student Teachers*. Larchmont, NY: Eye On Education, 2000.

📖 Rhodes, Immacula A., *Teaching with Favorite Back-to-School Books*. Monroe, NC: Scholastic Teaching Resources, 2004.

📖 Seldin, Peter, *How To Produce A Teaching Portfolio, 2nd ed.*, Boston: Anker Publishing Co.

📖 Wong, Harry K and Rosemary Tripi Wong, *The First Days of School: How to Be an Effective Teacher.* 2nd edition. Mountainview, CA: Harry K. Wong Publishing, 1998.

Journals and Magazines:

📖 **Better Teaching:** Teacher Institute; PO Box 397, Fairfax, VA 22039-0397; Phone: 703-503-5413

📖 **Instructor:** Scholastic Inc., 555 Broadway, 2nd FL, New York NY 10012-3999; Homepage: http://www.scholastic.com/inschool; Phone: 212-343-6220

📖 **NEA Today:** National Education Association, 1201 16th St NW, Washington, DC 20036; E-mail: NEAToday@aol.com; Phone: 202-822-7207

Internet Sites:

📖 **Education World,** http://www.educationworld.com (Search: back to school, search: icebreakers)

📖 **First Gov,** http://www.firstgov.gov/ (Search: Back to School)

📖 **Gradebook Software,** http://www.gradebookpower.com, using your computer to keep grades.

📖 **PBS TeacherSource,** http://www.pbs.org/teachersource, tips for starting the school year.

📖 **Pro Teacher,** www.proteacher.com

📖 **Secondary Educators,** 712educators.about.com (Search: Back to School)

📖 **Teachers Net Gazette,** http://teachers.net/gazette/

📖 **Teacher Tips,** tips to help start the school year http://www.nea.org (Search: Teacher tips)

📖 **The Teacher's Corner,** http://www.theteacherscorner.net (Select seasonal items.

📖 **Teaching,** http://www.unl.edu (Search: teaching, 101ways), 101 Things for the First 3 Weeks.

Chapter 3: Evaluation / Assessment

Evaluation and assessment (we will use assessment to refer to both in this chapter) are at the forefront of teaching. The expectations that teachers have for students, the objectives that are set as we plan and prepare for instruction must be guided by assessment. We must ask ourselves what we want our students to learn and then how will we know that they have learned it. Quizzes and tests are only one means of assessment. There is so much more that encompasses good assessment. The use of standardized testing has come under criticism today when it is used as the only means of evaluation to make important decision regarding students' retention, promotion, graduation, etc. In view of the findings regarding student learning by researchers such as Howard Gardner, we realize that students have different learning styles and it is worthwhile to consider that we may assess students in other ways besides paper and pencil or computer multiple choice answers!

We are going to explore a variety of alternatives for assessing your students. It is our desire that you will begin to think of assessment as a variety of tools that are not confined to multiple choice quizzes and tests.

Campbell's Law: "The more any quantitative performance measure is used to determine an individual's rewards, the more subject it will be to corruption pressures, and the more it will distort the action and thought patterns of those it is designed to monitor."

- Donald Campbell, past president, American Psychological Association

I. Closing the Loop

- Let assessment inform your instruction.

- In planning unit activities, plan what and how you will evaluate first.

- If students are having problems with quizzes and tests, reassess your teaching of the unit.

- Plan a variety of activities and a variety of ways to assess your students.

- Use pretests to determine if students have prior knowledge to help you find a beginning point for instruction.

- Do informal games or contests to determine students' progress and knowledge gained.

- If students are not grasping a concept, search for other ways to present the material.

- If you have a few students who have grasped a concept, allow them to explain in their own words to the class as a group or working individually with other students (whatever the students feel comfortable doing). Some times students find a way to put in understandable terms for their peers.

- When planning assessment, take into consideration the abilities and learning styles of all your students.

- If you are going to use multiple choice questions, matching, short essay, etc. on your tests, give students similar experiences with these formats on worksheets, etc., prior to the test situation.

"The farther you get away from real kids, the more you think standardized testing is a great idea!"

- Alfie Kohn,

II. Create Rubrics for Assignments

□ The first step for developing rubrics is to do unit planning and establish criteria for projects, products, writing, etc. that students will complete.

□ .Use the criteria and points given for assignments to establish, for example, what will suffice to earn 1 of 4 points; what will suffice to earn 2 or 4 points; 3 of 4 points, etc. for each objective.

□ Use spreadsheets or rubric creating software or rubrics' Internet sites (see resources at end of chapter).

□ Once you use a rubric, re-evaluate the criteria to see if it needs any alteration.

□ Teach students how to interpret rubric criteria so that they are clear about your expectations for an assignment.

□ Share with students your evaluation to help them comprehend your grading of an assignment with the rubric. This may help them to understand future rubrics.

□ If you change or add criteria to an assignment, be sure to change or add to the rubric.

□ Share assignments and rubrics that you develop with other same subject/grade level teachers. They may in turn share the assignments and rubrics they create.

□ Partner with another same subject or grade level teacher/teachers to develop a unit with assignments and rubrics.

□ Be sure that your rubrics measure what you intend and are fair to all.

III. Develop Your Own Quizzes and Tests

📖 Creating your own quizzes and tests allows you to be reasonably sure that you are assessing what you have taught.

📖 Use commercially developed quizzes and tests as a resource.

📖 Vary the types of questions you write yourself, but use standardized test formats of multiple choice to assist your students to be prepared for such testing.

📖 Use the Internet as a resource for developing quizzes and tests and finding other means of evaluation.

📖 Create answer sheets that are easy for you to score.

📖 Create answer keys and laminate or insert in sheet protectors for reuse.

📖 Create rubrics for higher level testing of essay, short answer questions, etc.

📖 You may want to make different versions if your students sit at tables or in close proximity during tests. Most test creator software is easy to use, allows you to type in questions that you may select for your test, and then scramble for different versions.

📖 Review quiz and test questions and delete or revise questions that are missed by the majority of your students.

📖 If your texts do not come with quiz-test creator software, you may want to invest in an inexpensive version. Also, there are some online sites for teachers to use for test creation.

📖 Date test versions you create and review periodically and update if necessary to insure that you cover any new content.

IV.   Utilize A Variety of Measurements

- Familiarize yourself with the concept of multiple intelligences by reading Howard Gardner's research.

- Provide musical options such as writing songs or raps for your criteria. Even allow for performance.

- Provide artistic options such as drawing, painting, and diorama within your evaluation criteria.

- Provide writing opportunities that vary such as a newspaper article, advertisement, letter, dialogue, poetry, play, defense, criticism, etc.

- Challenge students to create puzzles (crossword, matching, scrambles, etc.) for one another (limit amount for lower grades).

- Provide opportunities often for discussion that allows students to share opinions and ideas. Be open to all responses within appropriate parameters.

- Provide opportunities for presentations, with and without electronic slideshows.

- Encourage students to develop a study sheet, organizational diagram (chart, web, etc.) or other means to interact with study criteria and share with class. Encourage creative responses that may go outside of those you propose.

- If subjects lend themselves to debate, teach students rules for debate that will be necessary for respect and decorum. Let them take sides and prepare for a debate. Teach them to be sure to predict their opponents arguments and prepare to counter.

- Provide opportunities to experiment or make predictions and follow up with analysis and synthesis. Even if answers are not correct, much can be gained by the process.

V.   Teach Students To Take Standardized Tests

📖 Teach students to manage the stress of tests through deep breathing, stretching, standing up before beginning a test and shaking arms, etc.

📖 Teach student to listen and to read directions and testing material very carefully.

📖 Encourage students to check as they progress through a test that they are putting answers in the corresponding answer on answer sheet, etc.

📖 Encourage students to circle numbers of questions they want to come back to if they have time at the end of the test.

📖 Encourage students never to take too much time on one question. Ask them to circles numbers of questions that seem to take too much time to answer and come back to it at the end

📖 Teach student to cross off distracters they are certain are not correct answers so they can focus on less choices.

📖 Teach students to underline or highlight key information in a paragraph, question, etc.

📖 Teach students that some answers will require more than one step to solve.

📖 If guessing will not penalize participants, suggest consistent choices of B or C (2 or 3) to increase their chances of more correct answers.

📖 If guessing will penalize participants, encourage students to be sure that they skip non-answered on answer sheet, booklet, etc.

"Standardization, the great ally of mediocrity, wins out over imagination."
- Sergiovanni, educator, author

VI. Standardized Tests Versus Creativity

📖 Incorporate creativity in preparation for standardized tests.

📖 Example: Ask students to write a short story that has a surprise ending. Have students exchange papers and circle all nouns and X all verbs. Then have the students write a comment about the author's story.

📖 Example: Have students write math word problems for a math concept being studied. Share problems without revealing names. Try to solve. Discuss if it can or cannot be solved, why or why not. Students will get better and will maybe even realize why study math with practical applications they discover.

📖 Example 3: Have students put words with math problems to create fun words. 16 bananas + 19 apples = _____ banapples; 250 zebras / 30 rhinos = _____ zebnos or rhinbras.

📖 Example: Science teachers can reinforce language skills by asking students to write good hypotheses as well as grammatically correct hypotheses.

📖 Example: In Spelling have students write alliterations for spelling words. Challenge students to use all rhyming words for a few spelling words of their choice to make a sentence.

📖 Example: In social studies ask students to write "what ifs" for historical events insisting on correct grammar.

📖 Example: In language arts, read the beginning of a short story. Stop before the end and ask all students to write a prediction for the end of the story. Collect and finish story. Discuss their predictions. Next day, put sentences on overhead. Analyze sentences for grammar, spelling, etc. without revealing who wrote it. Discuss conversational and formal language.

VII. Group and Individual Evaluation

📖 When using groups, be sure everyone has a task they are responsible to do for the group. Use chart paper, color pens, color index cards, etc. as reminders that everyone must contribute.

📖 Give all students a group evaluation score and an individual score.

📖 Circulate during group work to facilitate and encourage participation of all group members.

📖 If using rubrics for individual and different rubrics for the group, share the criteria with all students.

📖 If you give a group quiz or test, use only individual scores and let students know they are only responsible for their own responses, not the group (in other words, they may agree to disagree).

📖 If students have prepared individual presentations, use the rubrics, making sure to have positive remarks as well as areas to improve.

📖 You may want to use rubrics occasionally to allow student evaluations for presentations, perhaps 2 (two) reviewers per presenter.

📖 You may want to give rubrics to each participant of a group and let them self-evaluate their group's performance.

📖 Get feedback from the whole class after a group assignment to get their feelings and to assess any miscommunications about group work or problems the groups encountered.

📖 Vary individual assignments to different groups for new group assignments to allow students to work with a variety of personalities and abilities.

"Too often we give our children answers to remember rather than problems to solve." - Roger Lewin, anthropologist and author

VIII. Testing Provisions for Exceptional Students

- Teach and encourage the use of all test taking strategies outlined for taking standardized tests.

- Allow exceptional students to take tests in another setting, such as in the media center with supervision, guidance counselor's office, etc. Be sure to ask permission to send the student at a particular time.

- Allow exceptional students to take tests with a longer time period.

- Require fewer questions to be answered by exceptional students. Perhaps even prepare a separate test with specific questions (easily done with word processing).

- Permit the student to have a reader for the test if reading is the area of need, preferably outside of the classroom during class testing. (However, usually may not provide for standardized reading tests).

- Teach all students quick organizers to help them analyze a problem or paragraph of information (outline, web, flowchart, highlighting, Venn diagrams, other types of diagrams, etc.).

- Provide lots of scrap paper for organizing, visualizing, figuring, etc.

- Print quizzes and tests in larger print versions for students with vision problems (quite easily done in word processing).

- Double-space paragraphs for students who have problems reading single spaced paragraphs (again, easily done in word processing).

- Promote a safe and relaxed environment for tests and always be available and alert during all testing, never seated at your desk.

"Everything that can be counted does not necessarily count; everything that counts cannot necessarily be counted." - Albert Einstein

IX. Recognize Good Versus Poor Evaluation

- If the majority of your students fail a quiz or test, consider throwing the quiz or test grades out and re-teaching and retesting.

- Use activities for review of material in class to predetermine students' readiness before a quiz or test.

- Avoid pop quizzes or pop tests, unless you really mean to trip up your students.

- If you are using commercially designed quizzes and/or tests, make sure you are covering all of the material that will be tested.

- Provide a variety of ways to measure student progress to address all of your students' strengths. Provide tests that have a variety of question types, again to meet the strengths of all your students.

- Ask students to write quiz or test questions, a good way for them to review the material. Whether you use the questions as they are or revise them, it will give you an idea what students have learned and what students anticipate you will test. If you and the students concur, great!

- Consider giving quizzes or tests that require listening skills. We seldom require such a test skill and yet it is a skill that is so valuable. It is a skill that many adults need to work on too.

- Consider giving quizzes or tests in a variety of ways: open note, open book, take home essay, group (another way to learn from others with discussion of questions), etc.

- When using rubrics, be sure they are evaluating the assignment accurately. If you have problems using the rubric, consider re-writing.

"Fairness is not an attitude. It's a professional skill that must be developed and exercised." - Brit Hume, news anchor

X. Communicating Evaluation to Students and Parents

📖 Inform parents of your grading policy (check school policy), important reports or other grading information for the school via introductory letters, handout to send home, etc. Send reminders and notices home periodically.

📖 Make sure to contact parents early in the school year on a positive basis so that communications about concerns are not your first contact.

📖 Communicate early in the school year that parent conferences, email, notes, etc. regarding grading, etc. are welcome.

📖 Review grading policies on a regular basis with students for projects, reports, etc. Meet one on one with a student at the first opportunity to discuss a failing grade on a quiz or test.

📖 Communicate via email, notes, phone, etc. to parents immediate concerns regarding student performance.

📖 Use a rubric and give students a copy of the rubric for their reference in preparing reports, projects, presentations, etc.

📖 Use the rubric to evaluate and share a copy of the evaluation with the student.

📖 Make anecdotal records of attempts to contact parents (copies of email, notes, etc.) as well as dates and times of one on one conferences with students and brief descriptions.

📖 Utilize grading conferences to praise students to parents for their successes before discussing concerns.

📖 Don't forget to call or email parents when students improve or with other good news.

"A child educated only at school is an uneducated child."
- George Santayana, philosopher, author

Notes

<u>Notes</u>

References and Resources

Books:

📖 Ball, Deborah Loewenberg, *Mathematical Proficiency for All Students: Toward a Strategic Research and Development Program in Mathematics Education.* Santa Monica, CA: Rand Publishing, 2003.

📖 Gronlund, Norman E., *Assessment of Student Achievement, 8th Edition.* Allyn and Bacon Publishing, 2005.

📖 Popham, W. James, *Classroom Assessment: What Teachers Need to Know, 4th Edition.* Allyn and Bacon, 2004.

📖 Stiggins, Richard J., Student-*Involved Assessment FOR Learning, 4th Edition.* Prentice Hall, 2004

📖 Books, Sue, *Poverty and Schooling in the US: Contexts and Consequences.* Mahwah, NJ: Lawrence Erlbaum Assoc., 2004.

📖 Cizek, Gregory J., Setting Performance Standards: Concepts, Methods, Perspectives. Mahwah, NJ: Lawrence Erlbaum Assoc., 2001.

📖 Nitko, Anthony J., *Educational Assessment of Students, Third Edition.* Des Moines, IL: Prentice Hall, Inc., 2001.

📖 Osler, Audrey and Kerry Vincent, *Girls and Exclusion: Rethinking the Agenda.* Mahwah, NJ: Lawrence Erlbaum Assoc., 2003.

📖 Sacks, Peter, *Standardized Minds: The High Price of America's Testing culture and What We Can Do To Change It.* Cambridge, MA: Perseus Publishing, 2000.

📖 Stotsky, Sandra, *What's at Stake in the K-12 Standards Wars: A Primer for Educational Policy Makers.* New York: Peter Lang Publisher, 2000.

📖 Vinson, Kevin D. and E. Wayne Ross, *Defending Public Schools*, Vol. 3. Westport, CN: Praeger Publishing, 2004.

📖 Zwick, Rebecca, *Rethinking the SAT: The Future of Standardized Testing in University Admissions.* New York: RoutledgeFalmer Publishing, 2004.

Journals and Magazines:

📖 **Childhood Education,** 17904 Georgia Avenue, Suite 215, Olney, MD 20832.   (800)423-3563,   (301)570-2111,   Fax: (301)570-2212 aceimemb@aol.com,: http://www.udel.edu/bateman/acei,

📖 **Curriculum Review,** 316 North Michigan Avenue, Suite 300, Chicago, IL 60601. 800)878-5331, (312)960-4100, EMAIL: cservice@ragan.com, INTERNET: http://www.ragan.com, Fax: (312)960-4106

📖 **Education at Issue,** PO Box 233, Woodtown, NJ 08098

📖 **Education Standard:** M I I Publications, 733 15th St NW Ste 900, Washington, DC 20005-2112; Phone 202-347-4822.

📖 **Educational Assessment,** 10 Industrial Avenue, Mahwah, NJ 07430. 973)236-9500, http://www.erlbaum.com/, Fax: (973)636-0072

📖 **Issues in Science and Technology,** PO Box 830688, MS AD13 Texas University, Richardson, TX 75083. (972)883-6325

📖 **Learning and Leading With Technology,** 480 Charnelton Street, Eugene,   OR   97401.   (800)336-5191,   (541)302-3777, cust_svc@ccmail.uoregon.edu,   http://www.isteonline.uoregon.edu,   Fax: (541)302-3778

📖 **Phi Delta Kappan**: P. O. Box 789, 408 N. Union, Bloomington, IN 47402. (800)766-1156, (812)339-1156, http://www.pdkintl.org, Fax: (812)339-0018

📖 **School Administrator,** 801 North Quincy Street, Suite 700, Arlington, VA 22203. (703)875-0748, membership@aasa.org, http://www.aasa.org, Fax: (703)841-1543

📖 **Teaching Children Mathematics,** 1906 Association Drive, Reston, VA 22091.   (800)235-7566,   (703)620-9840,   rdrake@nctm.org, http://www.nctm.org, Fax: (703)476-2970

📖 More online at **http://www.publist.com**

Internet Sites:

- **Developing Educational Standards** (connect to state standards), http://edstandards.org/Standards.html.

- **Discovery Education, Discovery School**. Select *Kathy Schrock's Guide for Educators, Assessment and Rubrics*. http://school.discovery.com/

- **Easy Test Maker**, free test generator, http://www.easytestmaker.com/default.aspx

- **FairTest: The National Center for Fair and Open Testing** (a variety of topics for assessment), http://www.fairtest.org

- **Landmarks for Schools**, Choose **Web Tools**, Choose **Rubric Builder** http://landmark-project.com/index.php.

- **National Educational Technology Standards Projects**, http://cnets.iste.org/

- **Rubistar for Teachers,** rubistar.4teachers.org Use to create rubrics for assessment.

- **TEACHERS.NET**: http://www.teachers.net/jobs/. Resource for finding K-12 positions, etc.

- **Teacher Vision** (Rubrics, lesson plans, graphic organizers, etc.) http://www.teachervision.fen.com/

- **Teachnology** (Select: Rubrics [scroll down]. Also dropdown menu by subject areas) http://www.teach-nology.com.

- **The Teachers Internet Use Guide** (Choose: Assessment) http://www.rmcdenver.com/useguide/

Chapter 4: Understanding Students and Subjects

Teachers need to know their subject but they also need to know how that subject relates to other subjects that are taught at the school. Teachers need to know and be able to show how their subject is relevant and useful to students now and in the future. Primary to this goal is an understanding of students, how alike and how different they are from one another. There are many aspects to what each individual student brings to the classroom and we will look at many research-based theories on development and learning theories. What teachers do today in the classroom and how they choose to teach their subjects is a result of many years of research. That research gives us the fundamental basis for the science of teaching. However, when the teacher absorbs that knowledge and begins to make it his/her own, that is when the magic begins and science turns into art.   To understand this is to observe in the classroom of several teachers in the same school. You will probably see many commonalities in the way that the classroom looks, but you will most assuredly observe many different teaching styles. If you observe elementary teachers and secondary teachers, you will observe many fundamental differences because of the level of the students. How amazing the difference a teacher can make to students and to the subject. It can be a wonderful exploration in which students become engaged in the safe and secure stewardship of a knowledgeable and understanding teacher.

"Instruction begins when you, the teacher, learn from the learner; put yourself in his place so that you may understand . . . . what he learns and the way he understands it."
- Kierkegaard, philosopher, author

I.   Hierarchy of Needs – Abraham Maslow

- 📖 Students who come to school hungry have difficulty focusing on lessons and learning

- 📖 Consider providing some minor comforts that may cost a little but will help those students whose needs are not being met (ex: breakfast bars, fruit snacks, sweater, pencils, hand lotion, etc.).

- 📖 Students with problems at home will have problems focusing on school and learning.

- 📖 Be available to your students, especially those who are struggling with behavior and academics.

- 📖 Students who are afraid cannot concentrate on learning.

- 📖 Make your classroom a safe environment where students feel welcome.

- 📖 Students whose classroom behavior suddenly changes may indicate that a need is not being met for that student at home.

- 📖 Speak with students whose behavior changes as soon as possible to determine if intervention is needed.

- 📖 Collaborate with the school nurse, physical education teacher, health teacher, etc. to offer time for discussion topics to provide coping strategies for various personal issues.

- 📖 Read books with or to students that facilitate discussions of changeable issues of families such as varying families, divorce, etc. as appropriate for your students. It helps students to understand that they are not alone in experiencing problems.

Resource: Boeree, Dr. C. George, **Personality Theories: Abraham Maslow, 1908-1970,**. Psychology Department, Shippensburg University, 2006.

II. Stage Development – Eric Erickson

- 📖 Elementary students are usually in the Erikson stage of **industry versus inferiority**. Students are compelled to learn new skills quickly or they feel incompetent, that they are failures.

- 📖 Middle/senior high students are in the Erikson stage of **identity versus role confusion**. Students are exploring and achieving their identity in gender roles, politics, religion, etc.

- 📖 Use strategies such as <u>scaffolding</u> to help students have frequent successes as they learn a new concept.

- 📖 Provide homework and classroom practice that reinforces and strengthens students' skills. This foundation will build a basis for the next learning step.

- 📖 Use **wait time** when asking questions to give young minds the necessary time to reflect before answering. Students should never be ridiculed when wrong.

- 📖 Practice **patience** with all students but especially the <u>struggling</u> learner. → need to do

- 📖 Give students opportunities to **express** their **opinion** safely and with acceptance of all views.

- 📖 Facilitate the establishment of classroom **rules** and **consequences** with the input of students.

- 📖 Establish early in the year that you will enforce the rules of the classroom and the school **impartially**.

- 📖 Solicit the help of a **guidance counselor** when students confide personal problems beyond the realm of the teacher's responsibility.

Resource: Socioemotional Development, Educational Psychology Interactive. Valdosta, GA: Valdosta State University. Available at http://chiron.valdosta.edu/whuitt/col/affsys/erikson.html

51

III. Cognitive Development – Jean Piaget

- Cognitive development does not coincide with chronological age. **Students, therefore, develop at different rates**.

- Piaget identified four stages: **sensorimotor**, **preoperations**, **concrete operations**, and **formal operations**. Most students begin school in preoperations and change to concrete operations in elementary school. Middle and senior high students move to formal operations. REMINDER: These stages vary by student.

- Students learn from their environment and **adapt** to it.

- Students **assimilate** when learning by taking in new information and applying it to existing schemes in response to a new situation.

- Students **accommodate** when learning by changing existing schemes in response to new situations.

- Students learn through **social transmission** by observing others. This is good to remember to help non-English speaking students.

- Plan units with lessons that are interesting and appropriate for the students.

- Provide opportunities for students to learn from one another through discussion or cooperative learning.

- Be aware of students learning stages and when it is appropriate to use preoperational, concrete or formal learning strategies.

- When working with struggling learners be sure to consider where they may be in their cognitive development.

Resource: Genetic Epistemology, Jean Piaget, 2005. Available at http://tip.psychology.org/piaget.html.

IV. Language Development – Lev Vygotsky

📖 Lev Vygotsky describes language development as being influenced by culture and interaction with parents, peers, etc.

📖 Model good language and encourage good language skills with students.

📖 Provide opportunities in the classroom for students to interact with one another as part of language development.

📖 Immerse students in vocabulary development by promoting interaction and daily use of new vocabulary.

📖 Plan to teach collaborative units integrated with other subjects that explore new vocabulary and how it relates to every day use.

📖 Prepare to teach collaborative units integrated with other subjects and classes that give students opportunities to explore other viewpoints beyond your classroom.

📖 Plan collaborative units with lower grades that give older students opportunities to be role models in discussions.

📖 Provide opportunities often for discussion that allows students to share opinions and ideas. Be open to all responses within appropriate parameters.

📖 Utilize cooperative learning strategies that allow students to interact and take on various roles within the group.

📖 Encourage students to practice listening, looking for patterns in problem solving and making sense of what they hear and read.

Resource   Lev   Vygotsky   (1896-1934).   Available   at http://starfsfolk.khi.is/solrunb/vygotsky.htm

V.   Multiple Intelligences – Howard Gardner

- 📖 Provide students with opportunities to listen, speak and write as learning experiences and assessment for those with **linguistic** strengths.

- 📖 Offer students opportunities to analyze problems and do investigations for those with **logical-mathematical** strengths.

- 📖 Encourage students to perform or compose music and support students' appreciation of music for those with **musical** strengths.

- 📖 Support students' need to move and involve the body to solve problems for those with **bodily-kinesthetic** strengths.

- 📖 Advance student exploration of patterns, space and confined areas for those with **spatial** strengths.

- 📖 Instruct students to discuss answers to who, why, how, for what purpose, when, and where for those with **interpersonal** strengths.

- 📖 Utilize discussion that encourages students to discuss personal feelings, fears, and purpose for those with **intrapersonal** strengths.

- 📖 Organize opportunities for students to classify plants, animals, and minerals for those with **naturalist** strengths.

- 📖 Employ Gardner's **multiple intelligences** as you write lesson plans, develop integrated units, create assignments and construct assessment.

All children can learn, you just have to find their strengths!

Resource: Smith, Mark K., **Howard Gardner, Multiple Intelligences and Education**. Encyclopedia of Informal Education, 2003. Available at http://www.infed.org/thinkers/gardner.htm

VI.   Social Modeling – Alberto Bandura

- Profit from the knowledge that students will imitate an admirable **role model** by providing yourself as a primary model.

- Partner a student with problem behavior to work with an admirable **peer role model**.

- **Read** to students about young people their own age who are good role models. Conduct follow up discussions about what made that person a good role model.

- Conduct discussions about people the students **admire** and ask them to determine what makes them admire this person (parent, grandparent, aunt, uncle, friend, etc.

- Use **verbal praise** as a reinforcer for students when they demonstrate a preferred behavior.

- Use **peer tutoring** to help struggling learners. Be sure that the peer tutor and the struggling learner have a friendly relationship.

- Be **fair** in administering **reprimands** and **consequences** to all students.

- Be **fair** in administering **praise** and **overlooking** small infractions.

- Try **to avoid extreme reactions** to any behavior in your classroom, especially if it is not warranted.

Resource: Bentley, Judy K. C., **Improving Behavior and Self-Efficacy Beliefs In the Classroom Through Cognitive-Behavior Modification**. Available at http://www.txstate.edu/edphd/PDF/selfefficacy.pdf.

VII. Taxonomies – Benjamin Bloom

📖 Keep a copy of the revised Bloom's Taxonomy in your planbook.

📖 Use verbs such as list, tell, define, match, select for lower level **knowledge** objectives and assessments.

📖 Select verbs such as compare, explain, order, discuss, describe for the next level of **comprehension** objectives and assessment.

📖 Provide for the third level of **application** by choosing verbs such as apply, modify, demonstrate, discover, produce, teach, chart.

📖 For the higher level of **analysis/synthesis** select verbs such as analyze, classify, illustrate, connect, contrast, and prioritize.

📖 The next higher level of **evaluation** requires such verbs as evaluate, recommend, debate, judge for objectives and assessment.

📖 The highest level of **creation** necessitates the use of verbs such as combine, invent, hypothesize, produce, imagine, predict for objectives and assessment.

📖 To foster **creativity** provide a variety of resources that promote student exploration such as videos, models, diagrams, charts, books, photographs, cartoons, tables, graphs, surveys, diagrams, questionnaires, poetry, puppets, and anything that will lend itself to teaching **critical thinking**.

📖 Research and utilize the **two additional domains** which include the **affective** (emotions) and **psychomotor** (physical).

Resource: Smythe, Kevin and Jane Halonen, **Using the New Bloom's Taxonomy to Design Meaningful Learning Assessments**. American Psycholological Association, 2006. Available at http://www.apa.org/ed/new_blooms.html#

VIII. Brain-Based Learning

- Believe that learning is **innate** and involves **conscious** and **unconscious processing**.

- Focus educational experiences on **students' interests**.

- Create a **non-threatening** learning environment that is **highly challenging**.

- Utilize **cooperative learning** to solve **realistic problems** to facilitate brain-based learning.

- Encourage students to continue their classroom learning **beyond** the **classroom** setting.

- Promote **active processing** of experience through acceptance of **varying solutions** to a problem.

- Avoid lecture and provide complex and challenging experiences.

- Arrange learning experiences that permit students to **explore** their environment **safely**.

- Be aware that in learning environments students experience both **focused attention** and **peripheral perceptions**.

- Give genuine and honest feedback beginning with positive statements.

- Remember that the brain is complex and a variety of learning strategies is important.

Resource: Caine and Caine, Brain-Based (Compatible Learning, Compiled by Annette Lamb, 2001. Learning, Eduscapes.com, available at http://eduscapes.com/tap/topic70.htm

IX. B. F. Skinner

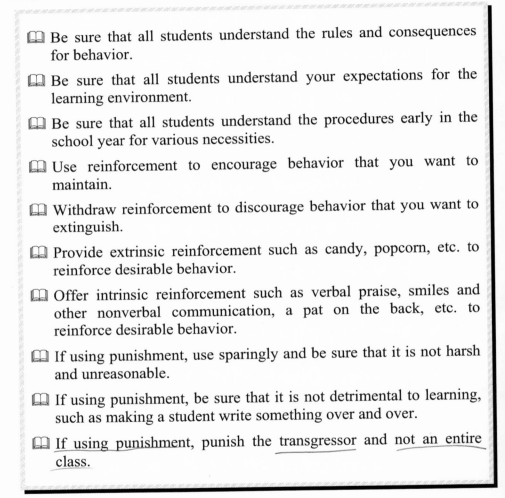

- Be sure that all students understand the rules and consequences for behavior.

- Be sure that all students understand your expectations for the learning environment.

- Be sure that all students understand the procedures early in the school year for various necessities.

- Use reinforcement to encourage behavior that you want to maintain.

- Withdraw reinforcement to discourage behavior that you want to extinguish.

- Provide extrinsic reinforcement such as candy, popcorn, etc. to reinforce desirable behavior.

- Offer intrinsic reinforcement such as verbal praise, smiles and other nonverbal communication, a pat on the back, etc. to reinforce desirable behavior.

- If using punishment, use sparingly and be sure that it is not harsh and unreasonable.

- If using punishment, be sure that it is not detrimental to learning, such as making a student write something over and over.

- If using punishment, punish the transgressor and not an entire class.

Resource: Instrumental Conditioning (Operant Conditioning), Fayetteville, AR: University of Arkansas, 2003. Available at http://www.uark.edu/misc/lampinen/PSYC2003_LEARNING.html

X.   Moral Development - Kohlberg

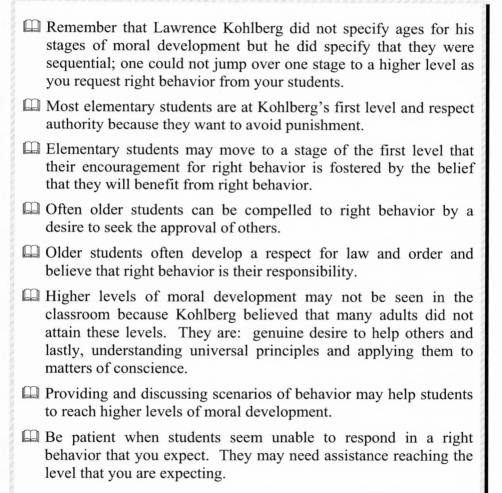

📖 Remember that Lawrence Kohlberg did not specify ages for his stages of moral development but he did specify that they were sequential; one could not jump over one stage to a higher level as you request right behavior from your students.

📖 Most elementary students are at Kohlberg's first level and respect authority because they want to avoid punishment.

📖 Elementary students may move to a stage of the first level that their encouragement for right behavior is fostered by the belief that they will benefit from right behavior.

📖 Often older students can be compelled to right behavior by a desire to seek the approval of others.

📖 Older students often develop a respect for law and order and believe that right behavior is their responsibility.

📖 Higher levels of moral development may not be seen in the classroom because Kohlberg believed that many adults did not attain these levels. They are: genuine desire to help others and lastly, understanding universal principles and applying them to matters of conscience.

📖 Providing and discussing scenarios of behavior may help students to reach higher levels of moral development.

📖 Be patient when students seem unable to respond in a right behavior that you expect. They may need assistance reaching the level that you are expecting.

Resource: Munsey, Brenda, Moral Development Moral Education and Kohlberg. Religious Education Press, 1980.

Notes

<u>Notes</u>

References and Resources

Books:

📖 Bandura, Albert, *Social Learning Theory*. Boston: Prentice Hall, 1976,

📖 Blakemore, Sarah-Jayne, *The Learning Brain: Lessons for Education*. Oxford: Blackwell Publishing, 2005.

📖 Bloom, Benjamin, *Developing Talent in Young People*. Ballantine Books, 1985.

📖 Devries, Rheta and Lawrence Kohlberg, *Constructivist Early Education, Overview and Comparison with Our Program: Overview and Comparison with Other Programs*. Washington D. C.: National Association for the Education of Young Children, 1989.

📖 Erikson, Erik H., *Identify and the Life Cycle*, Reissue. New York: W. W. Norton and Company, 1994.

📖 Gardner, Howard, *Frames of Mind: The Theory of Multiple Intelligences*. New York: Basic Books, 1993.

📖 Gardner, Howard, *Intelligence Reframed: Multiple Intelligences for the 21st Century*. New York: Basic Books, 2000.

📖 Jensen, Eric P., Brain-Based Learning: *The New Science of Teaching and Training, Revised Edition*. San Diego: Brain Store, 2000.

📖 Jensen, Eric P., *Brain-Compatible Strategies*. San Diego: The Brain Store, 2004.

📖 Maslow, Abraham H., *Toward a Psychology of Being, 3rd Edition*. Hoboken, NJ: Wiley Publishing, 1998.

📖 Munsey, Brenda, Moral Development: *Moral Education and Kohlberg*. Birmingham: Religious Education Press, 1985.

📖 Piaget, Jean, *Language and Thought of the Child*. Oxford: Routledge Classics: Routledge, 2001.

Skinner, B. F., *About Behaviorism.* New York: Vintage Publishing, 1976.

Shore, Rima, *Rethinking the Brain: New Insights into Early Development.* Families and Work Institute, 2003.

Journals and Magazines:

Current Issues in Education, College of Education, Arizona State University, P. O. Box 870211, Tempe, AZ 85287-0211. http://cie.asu.edu/

Education Standard: M I I Publications, 733 15th St NW Ste 900, Washington, DC 20005-2112; Phone 202-347-4822.

Environment and Behavior, University of Arizona, Sage Publications, 2455 Teller Road, Thousand Oaks, CA 91320; E-mail: info@sagepub.com

Journal of Experimental Psychology: Learning, Memory, and Cognition; 750 First Street, NE Washington, DC 20002-4242Fax (202) 336-5568; Phone (202) 336-5600; E-mail: subscriptions@apa.org.

New Teacher Advocate: Kappa Delta Pi, 3707 Woodview Trace, PO box 2669, Indianapolis IN 46268-1158; Phone: 317-871-4900

Next Step Magazine; PO Box 405, Victor, NY 14564-0405; E-mail: feedback@nextstepmag.com; Phone: 716-742-1260

Patterson's American Education: Educational Directories Inc.; PO Box 199, Mount Prospect, IL 60056-0199; Phone: 847-459-0605

Theory Into Practice: 169 Ramseyer Hall, 29 W. Woodruff Avenue, Columbus, Ohio 43210-1177; 614-292-3407; email – tip@osu.edu. http://www.coe.ohio-state.edu/tip/

More online at **http://www.publist.com**

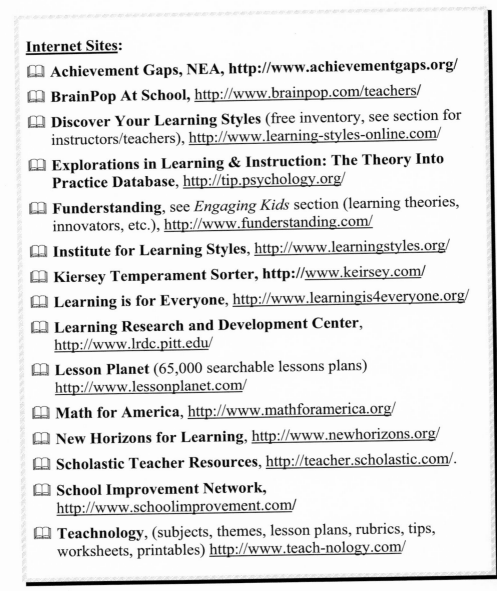

Internet Sites:

- **Achievement Gaps, NEA, http://www.achievementgaps.org/**
- **BrainPop At School,** http://www.brainpop.com/teachers/
- **Discover Your Learning Styles** (free inventory, see section for instructors/teachers), http://www.learning-styles-online.com/
- **Explorations in Learning & Instruction: The Theory Into Practice Database,** http://tip.psychology.org/
- **Funderstanding,** see *Engaging Kids* section (learning theories, innovators, etc.), http://www.funderstanding.com/
- **Institute for Learning Styles,** http://www.learningstyles.org/
- **Kiersey Temperament Sorter, http://**www.keirsey.com/
- **Learning is for Everyone,** http://www.learningis4everyone.org/
- **Learning Research and Development Center,** http://www.lrdc.pitt.edu/
- **Lesson Planet** (65,000 searchable lessons plans) http://www.lessonplanet.com/
- **Math for America,** http://www.mathforamerica.org/
- **New Horizons for Learning,** http://www.newhorizons.org/
- **Scholastic Teacher Resources,** http://teacher.scholastic.com/.
- **School Improvement Network,** http://www.schoolimprovement.com/
- **Teachnology,** (subjects, themes, lesson plans, rubrics, tips, worksheets, printables) http://www.teach-nology.com/

Chapter 5: Motivation and Critical Thinking

Teachers today experience the challenge of motivating students at all grade levels. Students today live in a world of stimulation through books, radio, television, computer programs, Internet websites, amazing visual and auditory effects of movies, realistic computer games and simulations, etc. It is important that teachers realize this because even though the student has a wealth of exciting resources, teachers also have these same resources available to them. As these tools become more and more common and more and more inviting, being aware of what students are exposed to through media, etc. is a very useful tool for teachers. As teachers we can effectively use these exciting resources as teaching tools and also teach students the limitations and the precautions to use when connecting to the world. As teachers we cannot turn our backs on the fact that the world is changing and we need to change with it. Teaching students exactly the same as someone did one hundred years ago is not going to motivate students to learn. "How frustrating to have to compete with the Internet," is a lament that some teachers make, but it is the reality of an ever changing world. As teachers, we are no longer the "bringer of all knowledge." The knowledge is available at the click of the mouse when students are connected to the Internet. **Research statistics tell us that the majority of students in the United States today have access to a computer at home or at school, so the digital divide has lessened.** Students should expect that their teachers will utilize the most current technology to teach them. The role of the teacher has evolved into "facilitator of knowledge." Helping students to explore their universe and knowledge is imperative. Teaching students to recognize false information or propaganda was never more important. The Internet has exposed our students to dangers that teachers and parents/guardians should teach our students how to avoid. We must demonstrate to our students that we understand the exciting world they live in and what we share with them is current and important to their future. Relevance of learning has become vital. You don't need to be an acrobat, singer, dancer, etc. to motivate students, just be willing to try new things!

I. Questioning for Critical Thinking

- Plan open-ended questions that must be answered with other than "yes" or "no."

- Use Bloom's Taxonomy of higher order skills as a basis for lesson objectives (analysis, synthesis and evaluation).

- Give students opportunities to find solutions to a problem that may vary from one another and demonstrate critical thinking.

- Ask students to write questions that do not have "yes" or "no" answers about a given topic.

- Ask students to do activities that require evaluation.

- Plan activities that provide opportunity for analysis.

- Give students the opportunity **to teach sections** of a topic, perhaps answering one of their own questions they submitted.

- Let students participate in the planning of evaluation of their learning by **making up test questions**, suggesting what vocabulary they all should be able to define, etc.

- Attempt to guide students to **expand upon the questions, vocabulary, evaluation**, etc. that they select when necessary.

- Plan lessons that allow students opportunities to hypothesize, synthesize, predict, experiment, reflect, apply, etc.

- Be supportive of the student's ideas and make every effort to be certain that all students have the chance to participate in planning, research, experiments, evaluations, etc. **(Ownership)**

"Think left and think right and think low and think high. Oh, the thinks you can think up if only you try!"
- Theodor Geisel, author, Dr. Seuss

II. Cooperative Learning Groups

- 📖 Assign students to groups that are similarly **balanced** by gender, race, abilities, etc.
- 📖 Teach students group dynamics so that they understand that **everyone needs to contribute** for the success of the group.
- 📖 With **cooperative learning** avoid establishing leaders of the groups so that students recognize that they are all equally important to the success of the group by assigning each a role.
- 📖 Prior to activities **explain how you will be grading**.
- 📖 Students should receive **individual as well as group grades**.
- 📖 **Monitor groups** to be sure that students are on task and that everyone is participating.
- 📖 Students who do not wish to function in a group **can accomplish the assignment individually** without retribution.
- 📖 **Students should be regrouped** from time to time in the same manner, perhaps after the completion of a given number of projects.
- 📖 Listen to complaints from students regarding the contribution of individuals to the group. **Take the individual aside to discuss solutions to the problem.**
- 📖 Plan a **variety of ways to evaluate the groups** so that you are encouraging the strengths of all of the individuals in each group.
- 📖 **Be prepared to experience a noisier classroom** because in order to be productive, the groups must communicate!

"Don't be afraid to let the students know that you're trying something new to make them powerful learners, and that you need their help."

Louis Schmier, Rule #14, Random Thoughts.
Madison, Wisconisn: Magna Publications, 1997

III.   Direct Instruction

- 📖 **Use attention getting devices** related to the lesson such as music, art, props, activities, poetry, short stories (one-page), sounds, a brief video, discussion, etc.

- 📖 **Demonstrate the skill**, breaking it down step by step, for the students.

- 📖 **Help the students to relate prior experience** to the lesson by soliciting discussion from the students or asking questions that prompt their memory.

- 📖 **Build upon skills that the students have already** learned and give them opportunities to practice the new skill.

- 📖 **Provide opportunities to practice the skill** with the teacher's guidance and then independently.

- 📖 As students practice the new skill, **circulate in the classroom to praise successful** applications and to correct any misconceptions.

- 📖 **Assess whether students have mastered the skill** before introducing a new skill.

- 📖 Assign homework only when you are **sure that the students can successfully complete it** independently.

- 📖 **Utilize homework to check mastery** and to catch misconceptions before they become a problem to be unlearned.

- 📖 Use performance-based evaluation that demonstrates the students' understanding **(authentic assessment).**

If you are planning for a year, sow rice;

If you are planning for a decade, plant trees;

If you are planning for a lifetime, educate people.

- Chinese Proverb

IV. Differentiated Instruction

📖 Plan to find out about your students' interests early in the year through a survey, questionnaire, etc. and utilize this knowledge throughout the school year as you teach.

📖 Encourage students to share what they already know about a topic to develop an understanding that we **learn from our experiences** and can expand upon our experiences.

📖 Be aware of the various learning styles in your classroom and provide opportunities continually for these various learning styles.

📖 Differentiate the content, process and/or product for the varying needs of the students in your classroom.

📖 **Encourage critical thinking skills** through discussion of topics that are open-ended and lend themselves to personal opinion.

📖 Learn to **ask open-ended questions** that help students to think in depth about a concept and perhaps prompt the students to ask their own questions.

📖 Avoid a "one size fits all" attitude when making assignments for students.

📖 Recognize that giving more advanced students *additional* work is not a means for differentiating instruction.

📖 When you plan to differentiate assignments, begin with an assignment that targets the average student, and then alter it to meet the needs of lower and higher ability students. The students will be doing the same basic assignment, only in varying degrees of difficulty.

V.   Discussion

- 📖 **Plan** questions to stimulate discussion of a particular topic.

- 📖 **Consider the ability of the students** that you are teaching when constructing questions for discussion.

- 📖 Plan questions that **promote higher levels of thinking** as opposed to simply asking students to recall data.

- 📖 **Use a seating chart that you can check off when you have called on a student** to answer a question or input their opinion or ideas to be sure that you include all students in discussions.

- 📖 When asking a question, **state the question before** you call upon a student to encourage everyone to listen to the question.

- 📖 In discussion lessons, learn to **guide reluctant students with questions that are more specific** and will help the student to reach an answer to a more complex question or concept.

- 📖 Stimulate thinking in discussion at times with **questions that challenge your students' minds.**

- 📖 **Provide a choice of answers** for students who seem unable to come up with a solution or idea.

- 📖 Use **wait time** to give students a chance to repeat a question in their minds and time to think through their answer.

- 📖 If discussion with a large group is unmanageable, consider first **breaking students into smaller groups** and circulate to facilitate group discussion. Then bring the groups together for a concluding discussion.

VI. Conceptual Learning

- Teach students problem solving techniques by testing a hypothesis together and modeling the techniques (**observation, scanning, identifying rules, testing, categorizing, classifying,** etc.).

- Teach students to structure hypothesis testing with **Venn diagrams, flow charts, diagrams, check lists,** etc.

- Teach students to use strategies in which they **observe the whole hypothesis to test it and eliminate possibilities,** or to select a part of the hypothesis and make changes to its other parts to test the hypothesis.

- **Begin with hypotheses that are easier to test** and solve and gradually introduce harder concepts.

- **Prepare a hypothesis (problem or abstraction) that you want your students to test** and any materials that they will need to test the hypothesis.

- **Plan how you will present the problem or abstraction** to motivate the students and involve them in the problem solving.

- **Let the students ask questions,** etc. to attempt to establish any patterns, etc.

- If students are having trouble with the problem or abstraction, **give them guidance with questions** for them to answer through observation to help them get started.

- Consider assigning students **to work in groups** to test the hypothesis.

- **Be lavish in your praise** of students' efforts and strategies used to test the hypothesis.

VII. Student Prepared Presentations and Other Student Involvement

- Within the given area of the curriculum, **solicit topics that the students would like to learn about.**

- Teach students (perhaps by doing an entire class project first) exactly **what comprises a presentation, debate**, **forum** or **panel** before attempting to utilize these strategies.

- **Begin with topics that are not very complicated** before selecting more complex and challenging topics.

- Vary the type of presentation that is used: **debate, forum, panel, computer presentation**, etc.

- **Begin with pairs or small groups and gradually work up to individually prepared activities** when students feel comfortable with the presentation format.

- Be flexible with seating arrangements **so students will have a good sightline** at all times.

- Promote **critical thinking** by being **open to students' responses** and encouraging students to **question** and **reflect**.

- Use **wait time** to be sure that students have enough time to think and reflect upon their experience before responding.

- Encourage students to **evaluate** their responses by **supporting** any statements that they make in the process of debate, etc.

- Be **supportive and encouraging of all students** making every effort to involve all students in this teaching strategy.

- Be supportive of the student's ideas and make every effort to be certain that all students have the chance to participate in planning, research, experiments, evaluations, etc. **(Ownership)**

VIII. Guest Speakers

⯃ First check your local and state guidelines regarding guest speakers. New laws in some states **require extensive screening**.

⯃ Choose **guest speakers** that compliment your curriculum and will be interesting to your students

⯃ Encourage guest speakers to bring **materials, animals, slides, video,** etc. to enhance their visit. (Be aware of school regulations.)

⯃ Encourage guest speakers to allow time for a question and answer period at the end of their presentation.

⯃ **Prepare** students by explaining your expectations of them before the visitor comes to the classroom.

⯃ **Re-contact guest speakers before their visit** to make sure that they have everything they need for their visit when they get to your classroom.

⯃ Although you prepare the students ahead of time, **make a planned introduction** of your guest speaker when they visit.

⯃ **Stay visible to your students** when the visitor is presenting.

⯃ Plan a **follow-up activity** that will emphasize and reinforce the visitor.

⯃ Plan time to have the students write **"thank you" notes** to the visitor.

⯃ Keep a record of **contact information** for successful guest speakers so that you can invite them again the next year.

Prepare a listening or questioning guide <u>with</u> students that they will use during the guest speaker's presentation.

IX.   Field Trips – Extensions of the Classroom

📖 **Before** a field trip, be **sure** to have all **necessary permission slips signed** and **in hand** before taking students off campus. **NEVER take a student without a permission slip.**

📖 When leaving the school campus, plan to have a **First Aid kit** and **emergency information about students**.

📖 Plan educational opportunities **related to your studies** to take students **outside the confines of the classroom**.

📖 Look around your **immediate community** for nearby, inexpensive field trips related to your curriculum. Many **businesses, stores, factories, restaurants, museums**, etc. welcome field trips by students.

📖 Examine your curriculum to take advantage of opportunities to take a class **outdoors** for **observation, writing, drawing,** etc.

📖 When traveling by bus, **plan activities for the bus ride** that are related to the content being studied. Prepare a sheet with directions and with lines on which the students can write the information you have requested.

📖 **Provide students with nametags** that also have the name of the parent/guardian responsible for them on the field trip.

📖 Be sure that parents/guardians are **aware of time allotment, meeting places,** etc. before leaving for the field trip.

📖 Write **"thank you" notes** and have the students write "thank you" notes to the parents/guardians who accompanied them on the trip.

📖 Visit a site that you plan to take students to on a field trip and **list the things that you would want the students particularly to see.** Provide this list for the parents/guardians the day of the field trip.

X.   Projects

- 📖 Utilize whole class and group projects to **model** approaches to such an assignment before assigning individual projects for students.

- 📖 Plan **open-ended project assignments** that lend themselves to and encourage the creativity of the students.

- 📖 Consider the **age and abilities of the students** and plan accordingly when making a project assignment.

- 📖 Provide the students with a **long list of possibilities** of ways that they can respond to the project assignment to help them get started.

- 📖 If you want to be sure that the students do the projects themselves, **provide as much time as possible** that the projects can be done in the classroom.

- 📖 Plan a day that parents/guardians can come into the classroom and work with the students to **help** them with projects.

- 📖 Early in the school year send a letter home to parents/guardians requesting donations of any materials that would lend themselves to projects, such as **straws, yarn, material scraps, wallpaper remnants, large pieces of cardboard, lightweight wire**, etc.

- 📖 **Plan a day to have visitors** (administrators, other classes, parents/guardians) come to view the projects.

- 📖 **Evaluate carefully** considering age, abilities, effort, etc. Remember to encourage creativity!

- 📖 Allow students an opportunity to **evaluate one another's projects** using predetermined criteria, perhaps limiting them to five projects. (Make sure everyone will be evaluated by a peer.)

<u>Notes</u>

<u>Notes</u>

References and Resources

Books:

📖 Barnard, Tony, *Mathematical Groups*. Lincolnwood, IL: NTC Publishing Group, 1996.

📖 Briggs, Dennie, *A Class of Their Own: When Children Teach Children*. Westport, Conn: Bergin and Garvey Pub., 1998.

📖 Cohen, Elizabeth G., *Designing Groupwork: Strategies for the Heterogeneous Classroom*. New York: Teachers College, Columbia University, 1994.

📖 *Creativity and Collaborative Learning: A Practical Guide to Empowering Students and Teachers*. Baltimore, MD: P. H. Brookes Publishing, 1994.

📖 Daniels, Harvey, *Methods That Matter: Six Structures for Best Practice Classrooms*. York, Maine: Stenhouse Publishers, 1998.

📖 Fry, Ronald W., *Last Minute Study Tips*. Franklin Lakes, NJ: Career Press, 1996.

📖 Fry, Ronald W., *The Great Big Book of How to Study*. Franklin Lakes, NJ: Career Press, 1999.

📖 *Giant Encyclopedia of Circle Time and Group Activities for Children 3 to 6*. Beltsville, MD: Gryphon House, 1996.

📖 Griswold, Robyn Hallowell, *Cooperative Learning Basics: Strategies and Lessons for U.S. History Teachers*. Amawalk, NY: Golden Owl Publishing, 1995.

📖 Gunter, Mary Alice, *Instruction: A Models Approach*. Boston: Allyn and Bacon, 1999.

📖 Jacobson, David, *Methods for Teaching: A Skills Approach*. New York: Merrill Publishing, 1993.

📖 Johnson, David W., *The New Circles of Learning: Cooperation in the Classroom and School*. Alexandria, VA: Association for Supervision and Curriculum Development, 1994.

📖 Kagan, Laurie, *Multiple Intelligences: Structures and Activities*. San Clemente, CA: Kagan Publishing, 2000.

📖 Robinson, Adam, *What Smart Students Know: Maximum Grades, Optimum Learning, Minimum Time*. New York: Crown Trade Paperbacks, 1993.

📖 Schmuck, Richard A., *Group Processes in the Classroom*. Dubuque, Iowa: William C. Brown Publishing, 1992.

📖 Strube, Penny, *Getting the Most from Literature Groups*. New York: Scholastic Professional Books, 1996.

📖 Thomas, Russell M., *Beating Boredom, Creating Interest*. Bloomington, Ind: Phi Delta Kappa Educational Foundation, 1997.

Journals and Magazines:

📖 **Arts and Activities**: Publishers Development Corp.: 591 Camino de la Reina, Ste 200, San Diego, CA 92108; **Phone**: 619-297-8032

📖 **Classroom Connect:** Wentworth Worldwide Media, 2221 Rosecrans Ave, Ste 237, El Segundo CA 90245-4954; E-mail: connect@classroom.com; Phone: 717-393-1000

📖 **Contemporary Education:** Indian State University, Statesman Towers, Rm 1005, Terre Haute IN 47809; E-mail: soeshiel@befac.indstate.edu; Phone: 812-237-2970.

📖 **Creative Classroom**: Creative Classroom Publishing LLC; 149 Fifth Ave, New York, NY; **E-mail**: ccmagedit@inch.com; 212-353-3639; Creative Classroom Publishing LLC, PO Box 53151, Boulder, CO, 80328-3151, United States

📖 **Elementary School Journal:** University of Chicago Press, Journals Division, Box 37005, Chicago IL 60637; E-mail: subscription@journals.uchicago.edu; Phone: 773-753-3347

📖 **English Education:** National Council of Teachers of English, 1111 W Kenyon Rd, Urbana IL 61801-1096; E-mail: rsmith@ncte.org; Phone: 217-328-3870

📖 **Innovations in Science Education and Technology:** Plenum Publishing Corp, 233 Spring St, New York NY 10013-1578; E-mail: info@plenum.com; Phone: 212-620-8000

📖 **Learning and Motivation:** Academic Press, Inc., 525 B St, Ste 1900, San Diego CA 92101-4495; E-mail: apsubs@acad.com; Phone: 619-230-1840

📖 **Mathematics Teacher:** National Council of Teachers of Mathematics, 1906 Association Dr, Reston VA 20191-9988; E-mail: orders@nctm.org; Phone: 703-620-9840

📖 **Media and Methods:** American Society of Educators, 1429 Walnut St., Philadelphia PA 19102; E-mail: michelesok@aol.com; Phone: 215-563-6005

📖 **Reading Improvement:** Project Innovation, Inc., 1362 Santa Cruz Ct, Chula Vista CA 91910-7114; Phone: 334-633-7802

📖 **Teaching for Learning:** Anderson-Shea, Inc., PO box 4780, Jackson WY 830001; E-mail: 72460.2362@compuserve.com; Phone: 307-734-8207

📖 **Science Teacher:** National Science Teachers Association, 1840 Wilson Blvd, Arlington VA 22201; E-mail: thescienceteacher@nsta.org

📖 **Teaching and Learning: The Journal of Natural Inquiry:** University of North Dakota, PO Box 7189, Grand Forks ND 58202-7189; Phone: 701-777-4421

📖 **What Works in Teaching and Learning:** Aspen Publishers, Inc., 7201 McKinney Circle, Frederick MD 21701-9782; E-mail: customer.service@aspenpubl.com; Phone: 301-417-7500

📖 More online at **http://www.publist.com**

Internet Sites:

📖 **Association for Direct Instruction,** information on direct instruction, http://www.uoregon.edu (Search Direct Instruction)

📖 **Cooperative learning**, principles of Cooperative Learning, http://www.excel.net (Search: ssmith, cooperative learning)

📖 **Critical Thinking Company: Empower the Mind**, http://www.criticalthinking.com/index.jsp

📖 **Daily Bite Educational Materials**, tools for effective teaching, http://www.dailybite.com/.

📖 **Internet For Classrooms**, Select *Links for K-12 Teachers*, http://www.internet4classrooms.com/

📖 **National Service-Learning Clearinghouse -** A Repository of Service Learning, http://www.nicsl.coled.umn.edu/.

📖 **NGA Center for Best Practices**, resource concerning best practices, http://old.nga.org (Search: Center for Best Practices, Activities)

📖 **One Computer, One Classroom,** making decisions about organizing learning experiences, http://discoversd.tie.net (Search: teacher, get started, one computer

📖 **ProTeacher:** new teachers, by subject, teaching practices, etc., http://www.proteacher.com/.

📖 **School Improvement Network**, select *Differentiated Instruction*, http://www.schoolimprovement.com/

📖 **TeacherVoices,** a real-time teacher-to-teacher chat room and message board service, http://www.teachervoices.com/.

📖 **The Innovative Classroom:** lesson plans, thematic units, etc., http://www.innovativeclassroom.com/.

📖 **Yahooligans!** Teacher's Guide: teaching resources, lesson plans, etc., http://www.yaholligans.com (Search: teacher's guide).

Chapter 6: Classroom Management

All GREAT disciplinarians are not necessarily GOOD teachers; however, all GREAT teachers are necessarily GOOD disciplinarians! -Anonymous

One of the most perplexing problems for new teachers (and many experienced ones) is the reality of classroom management. Like the above quote states, **keeping them "quiet" is not an indicator of "good" teaching.** While it is <u>necessary</u> to maintain a modicum of control to teach, **control should never be the "goal" or "aim"** of what you are trying to accomplish. This chapter illustrates a host of suggestions to aid you in maintaining a healthy teaching environment. However, good management is not a "bag of tricks," a "recipe," or a series of "nuts and bolts" one just need apply to solve all issues. **Rather classroom management is the compilation of four principles that act as filters the teacher utilizes to apply a technique, method or solution.** These principles must be well thought out initially and then continue to evolve as one's teaching career matures, they are:

I.   <u>Philosophy</u> - **WHY you have become a teacher.**

II.   <u>Personality</u> - **WHO you are (defining personal traits).**

III.   <u>Character</u> - **WHAT you believe (motivation, thoughts and ideals).**

IV.   <u>Talents</u> - **HOW you teach (Abilities which set you apart, such as: athletic--artistic--musical--written--verbal--etc.)**

I. Be Prepared and Well Organized

- Plan **short** and **long range goals** before school starts.

- Have a **planbook Monday morning** with well-developed plans for the week

- Make it a habit to **develop an outline** for the **following week**, if possible, when writing lesson plans for the week.

- **Over plan** lessons so that you may carry them over to another day or week.

- **Acquire** a repertoire of **meaningful activities** that lend themselves to a **variety** of **subjects**, such as relays at the chalkboard, bees, ongoing reading aloud of related books, etc.

- Have a **place** for **everything** and everything in its place; students need to be informed regarding this regulation.

- Change hardcopy **files** to **disks/zip drives or CD ROMs** ... if you like to handle less paper in the file cabinet then keep important information saved **electronically** with subject, etc.

- Organize materials for lab demonstrations, etc. **(in the afternoon before the lesson)** use plastic bins, for example, to have teaching materials ready at your fingertips.

- Organize file cabinets so that you can locate information quickly.

- Develop a **substitute folder** or **binder** with **pockets** that contain **duplicate copies** of **interesting** seatwork **relevant** to your subject matter: **seating charts, attendance sheets** to check, **general plans** that will be easy to follow, but may vary from what you are teaching at the time, etc. At least provide information as to where to **locate** these things.

II. Maintain a Sense of Humor

- 📖 **Smile,** it is **contagious.**
- 📖 **Read aloud** a **humorous book** to your students (yes, all ages).
- 📖 Look for **humorous anecdotes** that you can **share** with **colleagues.**
- 📖 Look for **humorous anecdotes** that you can **share** with **students.**
- 📖 **Do not take yourself so seriously** that you let children offend you with their frankness.
- 📖 **Search** for the **good** in **all** the **students** that you teach.
- 📖 Utilize **humor** in **teaching,** such as; writing limericks, students draw political cartoons, mixed up combinations of animals (elepharoo, a hopping elephant with a pouch), etc.
- 📖 Many **potential discipline problems** can be diffused by a **humorous** comment or action that does **NOT involve demeaning** the student.
- 📖 **Laugh with children, not at them.**
- 📖 <u>Avoid</u> colleagues that **lack humor** and are **negative.**

The teacher gave her third graders a lesson on magnetism and its properties. After the lesson, she began to ask questions.

"My name starts with an 'M,'" she told one little boy, "and I pick up things. What am I?"

Without hesitation, the lad replied, "A mother!"

P. Susan and Steven R. Mamchak, *Educator's Lifetime Library of Stories, Quotes, Anecdotes, Wit, and Humor*. West Nyack, NY: Parker Publishing Company, Inc, 1979.

III. Student Ownership

- Allow students to help in designing **classroom rules** the first day.
- Assign **student responsibilities** on a weekly or monthly basis.
- Discuss **student interests** and try to incorporate them into your lesson plans for subjects that lend themselves to this.
- Discuss a topic with students at the beginning of a unit to find out what they would like to learn about the topic.
- **Vary your style** of teaching to allow students greater opportunities to participate in activities in the classroom.
- Display student work on walls, bulletin boards, hallways, creative writing books, etc.
- Look for contests and such to encourage your students to enter.
- Encourage students to **help one another** and even encourage some talking to one another that is constructive.
- Encourage **self-discipline** by requiring personal maintenance of classroom rules and procedures.
- Communicate regularly your **expectations** of students and your desire for a classroom "community."
- Occasionally, place a rule breaker in charge of the rule they broke!
- When possible, meet with small groups of students (such as officers of the choir, band, orchestra, etc) to plan activities, programs, fundraisers, projects, etc.

IV. Teach to All the Learning Styles

- 📖 Read **educational texts**, **journals**, **articles**, etc. to discover what is new and innovative in the presentation of classroom material.

- 📖 Take a **class** for professional hours in learning **styles** and **methods**.

- 📖 **Brainstorm** with your colleagues about new things to try to motivate students.

- 📖 Seek out **inservices** or *workshops* that will present new methods or techniques.

- 📖 **Vary assignments** and provide **choices** of assignments, such as, long range projects might be accomplished in a variety of ways (song, rap, poetry, computer product, art, music, web page, letter, publication, constructed product, sewing, cooking, animal, vegetable, or mineral, etc.).

- 📖 Bring in **guest speakers** (family, friends, neighbors, parents/guardians of students, community workers, business people, medical professionals, local professors, writers, actors, veterinarians, agriculturalists, computer experts, etc.)

- 📖 **Share** your **talents** with another teacher's class as he/she shares his/her talent with your class.

- 📖 **Read aloud** a book to students of **any age** concerning the subject or unit that you are teaching.

- 📖 **Immerse** your students in a unit of study by planning with other teachers' ways to incorporate their subject into the unit.

- 📖 Examine **Internet web sites** for **quality multimedia presentations** online for topics that you teach and share with students

V.   Address the Behavior and Reject the Behavior

- Be **selective** in the behavior that you will **ignore** and the behavior that **cannot** be ignored.

- Develop the ability to **truly observe** what is happening in your **classroom** so that you are fair to your students.

- Have **pre-determined consequences** for behavior and be consistent in applying it.

- To address unacceptable behavior, **take** the **student aside privately**, away from the hearing of other students.

- **Listen** to the student to determine what **they believe** happened.

- **Establish** with the student that the **behavior** was **inappropriate**.

- Discuss with the **student** what he/she can do to **change** his/her **own behavior** that you observed.

- Help the student to understand that you **disapprove** of the **actions**, that you **are not disapproving of them**.

- **Avoid outbursts** or **angry words** that cannot be retrieved (count to ten slowly, breathe deeply, pick up a pen and paper and start writing what happened, clap your hands, flick the light switch, walk back and forth quickly hands clasped behind your back, do jumping jacks and order your students to join you, blow into a whistle or recorder, etc.)

- **Call parents/guardians** as soon as possible; involve the **principal** only as a **last resort**.

VI.　Be Fair and Consistent

📖 **Every day**, from the first to the last day of school, **every student** should be **expected** to **follow** the same **rules**.

📖 Be fair and **look honestly** for **good behavior** from every student.

📖 Make **NO assumptions** about who did what because of **prior incidents**.

📖 Be sure that **consequences** are **fitting** for the behavior.

📖 Consider using **peer intervention** to help diminish **disagreements** between students.

📖 Apply pre-determined **consequences** on an **equal basis** to all.

📖 Be **selective** in what you **ignore**, but especially be **consistent** with all students.

📖 **Punish individuals,** never the whole class.

📖 Do **NOT** take student behavior **personally**; we all have our "bad" days.

📖 **Model** adult behavior and expectations for your students by **NOT** using corporal punishment.

Remember that students will rise or fall

to your level of expectations!

VII. Positive Reinforcement: Catch Them Being Good

- Smiles, kind words, pats on the back, firm handshakes, written comments, applause, special bulletin boards recognizing students, are just a few **ways** to **communicate** that they are **great**.

- **Create** and use **simple certificates** that can be **filled out quickly** to remind students that you appreciate their good behavior.

- Create a **newsletter** to send home that points out all the great things the students have been doing, recognize special events or student accomplishments, etc.

- Recognize **birthdays**, all ages!

- **Tell** your students when you are **proud** of them.

- **Invite** parents/guardians, the principal, vice principal, counselor, etc. **into the classroom** frequently to **show off** projects, plays, artistic creations, murals, poetry, choral readings, debates, singing, experimental results, class contest results, class math competitions, spelling bees (root for the speller as much as the athlete!), videotaping, cassette recordings of students, etc.

- **Call parents/guardians** to say a **good word** about their student in your class.

- Plan an **awards time** to give **every student** a **certificate** for something good they accomplished during the grading period.

- **Plan** rewards for your students for good behavior, such as, popcorn parties, a movie one afternoon, coupons for free homework days, extra time at the computer, extra recess, etc.)

📖 Create a **bulletin board** for the **Student of the Week or Month** and recognize that student that week, such as, first to line up all week, buy or bring them lunch on Friday or eat-with-the-teacher-day, no homework, extra computer time, etc.

VIII. Be Definite

- The very first day of school when you make rules with your students, have **definite rules** that **you need** and **guide** your **students** toward them.

- Learn that you may definitely **NOT know everything**, but be definite that you and your students can **find** that **information**.

- **Never argue** with a **student**, be definite that you are the **teacher**, the **adult**.

- Be definite that you will **NOT accept less** than your expectations for behavior or achievement from your students.

- Be definite with **parents/guardians concerning student behavior** and what you will NOT accept.

- Be definite that **changing desk assignments** on a **regular basis** is good for all concerned.

- Be definite that you have your **own teaching style** and do NOT have to be just like anyone else.

- Be definite that **your students can learn**; however some may choose NOT too.

- Be definite that classroom management is **your responsibility**.

- Be definite that each day you **improve** as you **learn from experience**.

IX. Enlist Support

📖 Keep a **record** of **unacceptable** behaviors (persons involved, date, time, activity, etc.), what actions you have taken, how they have been received, etc., for **future reference** in calling upon others for their support.

📖 Solicit **objective opinion** from the counselor or other professionals concerning particularly troubling behavior and discuss **ideas** for dealing or coping with the behavior.

📖 Talk to experienced **colleagues** concerning a specifically troubling ongoing **discipline** problem.

📖 Call or email **parents/guardians** and **request** a **conference** regarding an ongoing discipline problem.

📖 **Write** down a written **plan** to **share** with **parents/guardians** concerning your **future actions** for this behavior and communicate this to them.

📖 Solicit from the **parents/guardians** a **plan of action** on their part regarding the ongoing discipline problem.

📖 **Communicate** to the **student** what your **future actions** will be and hope that the parents/guardians do likewise.

📖 Using the school guidelines, request **verbally** and/or in **writing** that a troubled student receive **counseling**.

📖 Request a **second conference** with **parents/guardians, principal, counselor**, other **teachers** of the student who experience similar behavior, etc. if nothing is accomplished regarding the behavior in a **reasonable** period of **time**.

X.   Conspiring To Do Good

- 📖 Join or begin a **faculty support group** specifically for the purpose of **opportunities** to **talk** about **discipline** problems and help one another be objective and feel upheld

- 📖 Begin all parent/guardian conferences on a **positive note**. Always emphasize that your main purpose is to help their child (your student) learn and grow.

- 📖 **Attend extracurricular activities**:   Football, Volleyball, Basketball, Baseball/Softball, Track, Tennis, Plays, Concerts, etc … in other words be visibly interested in the lives of your students outside of the classroom.

- 📖 **Volunteer**: coach a sport, sponsor an organization, advise a club.

- 📖 Interact **positively** with students when conducting **cafeteria duty, hall duty, bus duty, etc.** Do not begrudge being assigned a duty; utilize it as an opportunity to reach out to students in an informal atmosphere.

- 📖 Become active in **civic organizations**; e.g. Rotary, Kiwanis, Boy/Girl Scouts, etc.

- 📖 Become active in the church, synagogue, mosque, etc. of your choice.

- 📖 With the school's permission, and full acknowledgement of the parents/guardians, make occasional **home visits**. However, do not go alone. This is both a safety and legal precaution.

- 📖 **Spend thirty minutes before or after** school helping students with assignments. Be sure that ALL students know this time slot is there for help.

- 📖 **Go toward the problems**, not away form them!

<u>Notes</u>

Notes

References and Resources

Books:

📖 Ayers, William, *To Teach: The Journey of a Teacher*. New York: Teachers College Press, 1993.

📖 Banks, Stephen R., *Educational Psychology: For Teachers in Training*. Minneapolis, MN: West Publishing Co., 1995.

📖 Baron, Eleanor B., *Discipline Strategies for Teachers*. Bloomington, IN: Phi Delta Kappa Educational Foundations, 1992.

📖 Bean, Reynold, *Individuality, Self-Expression and Other Keys To Creativity*. Santa Cruz, CA: ETR Associates, 1992.

📖 *Beyond Behaviorism: Changing the Classroom Management Paradigm*: Boston: Allyn and Bacon, 1999.

📖 Charles, C. M., *Building Classroom Discipline*. New York: Longman Publishing, 1999.

📖 *Classroom Management for Secondary Teachers*. Boston: Allyn and Bacon, 1997.

📖 Evertson, Carolyn M., *Classroom Management for Elementary Teachers*. Boston: Allyn and Bacon, 2000.

📖 Frieberg, H. Jerome, *Universal Teaching Strategies*. Boston: Allyn and Bacon, 1992.

📖 Froyen, Len A., *Classroom Management: The Reflective Teacher-Leader*. New York: Macmillan Publishing, 1993.

📖 Glasser, William, *The Quality School Teacher*. New York: Harper Perennial, 1998.

📖 Gruber, Barbara, *100% Practical Ideas, Information, Strategies for K-6 Teachers*. Torrance, CA: Frank Schaffer Publications, 1993.

📖 Jacobsen, David A., *Methods for Teaching: Promoting Student Learning*. Upper Saddle River, NJ: Merrill Publishing, 1999.

📖 Loomans, Diane, *The Laughing Classroom: Everyone's Guide to Teaching With Humor and Play*. Tiburon, CA: H. J. Kramer Publishing, 1993.

📖 MacKenzie, Robert J., *Setting Limits in the Classroom: How to Move Beyond the classroom Dance of Discipline*. Rocklin, CA: Prima Publishing, 1996.

📖 Marshall, Marvin, *Discipline Without Stress Punishments or Rewards: How Teachers and Parents Promote Responsibility and Learning*. Los Alamitos, CA: Piper Press, 2001.

📖 McMullen, Avis, *Teaching in Perspective*. Hazelwood, MO: Word Aflame Press, 2000.

📖 Nathan, Amy, *Everything You Need to Know About Conflict Resolution*. New York: Rosen Publishing Group, 1996.

📖 Prosise, Roger D., *Beyond Rules and Consequences for Classroom Management*. Bloomington, IN: Phi Delta Kappa Educational Foundation, 1996.

📖 Simpson, Carolyn, *Coping Through Conflict Resolution and Peer Mediation*. New York: Rosen Publishing Group, 1998.

📖 Thompson, Julia G., Discipline *Survival Kit for the Secondary Teacher*. West Nyack, NY: Center for Applied Research in Education, 1998.

📖 Tompkins, James R., *Surviving in Schools in the 1990's*. Landham, MD: University Press of America, 1993.

📖 Wolfgang, Charles H., *Solving Discipline Problems: Methods and Models for Today's Teachers*. Boston: Allyn and Bacon, 1999.

Journals and Magazines:

📖 **Behavioral Educator:** Theodore A. Hoch, 509 Allen Hall, West Virginia University, Box 6122, Morgantown WV 26506-6122; Phone: 212-734-8401

📖 **Cooperative Education Association Newsletter:** 8640 Guilford Rd, Ste215, Columbia MD 21046-2615; Phone: 410-290-3666

📖 **Teaching Tolerance:** 400 Washington Avenue, Montgomery AL 36195; Homepage: http://www.teachingtolerance.org; Phone: 334-264-0286

📖 More online at **http://www.publist.com**

Internet Sites:

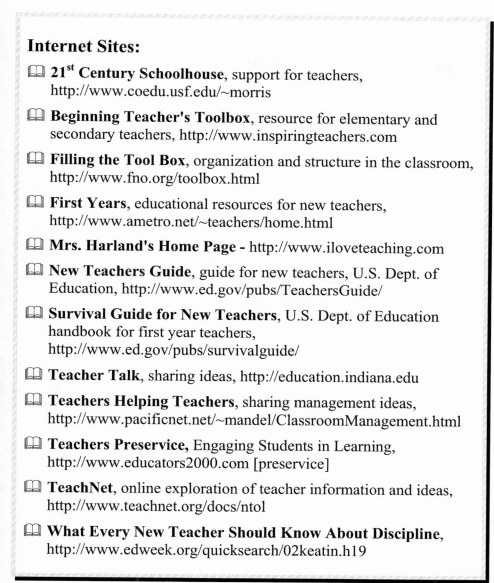

- **21ˢᵗ Century Schoolhouse**, support for teachers, http://www.coedu.usf.edu/~morris

- **Beginning Teacher's Toolbox**, resource for elementary and secondary teachers, http://www.inspiringteachers.com

- **Filling the Tool Box**, organization and structure in the classroom, http://www.fno.org/toolbox.html

- **First Years**, educational resources for new teachers, http://www.ametro.net/~teachers/home.html

- **Mrs. Harland's Home Page** - http://www.iloveteaching.com

- **New Teachers Guide**, guide for new teachers, U.S. Dept. of Education, http://www.ed.gov/pubs/TeachersGuide/

- **Survival Guide for New Teachers**, U.S. Dept. of Education handbook for first year teachers, http://www.ed.gov/pubs/survivalguide/

- **Teacher Talk**, sharing ideas, http://education.indiana.edu

- **Teachers Helping Teachers**, sharing management ideas, http://www.pacificnet.net/~mandel/ClassroomManagement.html

- **Teachers Preservice,** Engaging Students in Learning, http://www.educators2000.com [preservice]

- **TeachNet**, online exploration of teacher information and ideas, http://www.teachnet.org/docs/ntol

- **What Every New Teacher Should Know About Discipline**, http://www.edweek.org/quicksearch/02keatin.h19

Chapter 7: Dealing With Stress

Stress is not bad! Not managing stress is bad. Left unchecked, stress can lead to burnout. One of the most significant reasons, if not the most significant, that teachers leave the profession is **BURNOUT!** Nearly thirty percent of new teachers leave the field within their first five years of teaching. Additionally, the United States spends **BILLIONS** of dollars each year treating stress disorders. Because teaching is an important profession with a great deal of responsibility, stress levels tend to run very high. **If teaching were not an important profession, the stress level would be very low**. The first step all teachers must take in regard to stress is to recognize the **stressors** ... (undisciplined students, mundane duties, large class size, unmotivated students, demanding parents/guardians, unreasonable administrators, inadequate reward system, etc.). Secondly, teachers must be aware of the **burnout symptoms**. They usually occur in combination (sleeping and/or eating disorder, prolonged anger and/or depression, inability to concentrate, paranoia, sense of worthlessness, physical dysfunctions, etc.). In addition, the symptoms will be a change in the normal flow of one's life and new patterns of behavior emerge. This chapter outlines numerous **strategies (professional and personal)** for handling stress and avoiding burnout. Naturally, not all suggestions are for everyone, however, there are enough tactics listed within this chapter to assist one in gaining the upper hand in dealing with stress. **It is really up to you ... remember** *STRESSED* **spelled backwards is** *DESSERTS!*

I.   Communication

- Become a **good listener - Practice Active listening!**

- Discuss **classroom rules** and **procedures** with **students** the **first day** and be **consistent** in upholding them.

- When **talking** to **students** about their **behavior, concentrate** on the **behavior** and **NOT** on **personal criticism** of the **student**.

- **Take time, make time** to talk with your spouse, **significant others** and your children.

- **Choose** to talk with **colleagues** who are <u>**positive**</u> and make you feel **good** (avoid the teachers' lounge).

- Keep a **personal journal** that you record a **short paragraph** about your **feelings** at the end of **each day**.

- **Record** incidents concerning behavior, especially **stressful student behavior, immediately**.

- Contact **parents immediately** when there is a **problem** with a student. Beat the problem home!

- Make an appointment and discuss **serious dilemmas** with **administrators**.

- **Read** and **write** for personal enjoyment.

> I am not so much concerned with the right of everyone to say anything he pleases as I am about our need as a self-governing people to HEAR everything relevant.
>   -   **John F. Kennedy in a speech April 16, 1959**
> **Daniel B. Baker, *Power Quotes*. Detroit: Visible Ink Press, 1992**

II. Health, Nutrition and Exercise

- Go to your physician for a **yearly physical.**

- **Establish** an **exercise routine three** to **four times** a **week** that you **enjoy** and that does **NOT** leave you in **pain. (e.g.** walking, tai chi, yoga, nonimpact aerobics, etc.) Check with your physician when starting such a program of exercise.

- Eat **breakfast** to help you start the day refueled.

- Eat a well **balanced diet** that includes all six of the food groups.

- **Avoid excess weight** but do **NOT obsess** with weight either.

- If you must **diet**, discuss a **reasonable** diet with your **physician.**

- Be kind to your **feet**, invest in **quality shoes** that **fit well** and are **comfortable.**

- **Lift correctly** and **protect** your **back** from strain, a common problem for many people.

- Exercise your **mental capabilities** in ways you **enjoy**, such as, reading, puzzles, music, writing, poetry, games, discussions, etc.

- Do **NOT abuse tobacco, drugs** (prescription or over the counter also) or **alcohol.**

Our life is what our thoughts make it.

- Marcus Aurelius
Meditations, (161-180AD)

III.   Network and Support

- Develop a **mentoring relationship** with a **colleague** (new faculty especially).

- Be a **positive role model** and share **"good words"** with your **colleagues**.

- **Subscribe** to at least **one professional journal**.

- Yearly **expand** a **list** of people who **enjoy helping** out in your classroom, such as, assisting with projects, sharing a skill or personal knowledge, displaying their talents, etc.

- **Contact parents early** and **positively** and garner their **support** by showing that **you care** about their students in your classroom.

- **Team teach** with willing colleagues for variety and **sharing** your personal **special skills**.

- **Seek** the help of **resource people** such as the counselor, reading specialist, special education resource person, etc.

- Show your support by being an **active member** of your school's **parent-teacher organization**.

- Join or begin a **support group** for yourself and your colleagues. Join a **professional organization** for teachers.

- Be **aware** and **supportive** of your **colleagues'** successes, special events in their lives, problems, illnesses, travel, etc.

Be a Friend to Have a Friend.

IV. Diversions

- 📖 Develop a **sense of humor** and use it **frequently**.
- 📖 Take **mini vacations** on **weekends,** such as, visiting a nearby city and spending the night. Go to dinner and a movie and don't think about school.
- 📖 Change **grade levels** or change **subjects** at the end of the school year.
- 📖 Consider the possibility of changing **schools** at the end of the school year.
- 📖 Lose yourself in a **book** of your choice.
- 📖 Spend time with a **pet** that adores you.
- 📖 **Vary** your **teaching style** and try group projects, computer presentations, etc.
- 📖 **Reward** and **treat yourself** from time to time with money you have budgeted for such occasions.
- 📖 Take a **class** to **learn something** you have always wanted to learn that is **unrelated** to teaching.
- 📖 **Worship** in the faith of your choice.

MOST PEOPLE ARE ABOUT AS HAPPY AS THEY MAKE UP THEIR MIND TO BE. 😊

- ABRAHAM LINCOLN

V. Time Management

- 📖 **Handle** each piece of **paper only <u>once</u>.**

- 📖 **Generate** as **little paperwork** as possible.

- 📖 Make a **prioritized to-do list** every day and cross things off as you accomplish them.

- 📖 Have a **"place for everything and everything in its place."** Communicate this to students.

- 📖 Find **alternatives** to **grading** every paper.

- 📖 Learn to **say "NO."**

- 📖 **Delegate responsibilities** whenever reasonable to students, aides, or parents.

- 📖 Always consider **"waiting time"** as a **"gift of time"** to use positively, not fretting.

- 📖 Be **flexible** and expect the unexpected.

Little drops of water, little grains of sand,

Make the mighty ocean and the pleasant land;

Thus the little minutes, humble though they be,

Make the mighty ages of eternity!

- Julia Fletcher Carney
Carolyn Warner, *Treasury of Women's Quotations.* Englewood Cliffs, NJ:
Prentice Hall, 1992, pg. 296

VI. Humor and Hobbies

- Look for humor in the classroom, and **laugh** when it is **appropriate**. Laugh with your students, not at them!

- Use humor to **diffuse small problems** in the classroom, reserve seriousness for the big ones.

- Find **humorous books** to **read** to **students** (**all** age levels) to share humor with your students.

- **Model** for your **students** that there is a time to be funny, and a time to be serious to **help** them **recognize** that we have time for **both** in our lives.

- **Record humorous events** or **something funny** a **student said** in your **journal** at the end of the school day.

- Watch **humorous shows** or **videos** to unwind, as a break from tension.

- Acquire a **hobby** that you truly **enjoy** (art, cooking, ceramics, writing, remodeling, sewing, knitting, woodworking, camping, mountain climbing, etc.)

- Listen to **music**, and if your principal is agreeable, **soothe students'** seatwork time with soft, melodic sounds.

- Learn to play a **musical instrument**.

- **Smile** at those around you and it will return to you tenfold.

Jump into the middle of things, get your hands dirty, fall flat on your face, and then reach for the stars.

- **Joan L. Circio**

- **Carolyn Warner,** *Treasury of Women's Quotations.* Englewood Cliffs, New Jersey: Prentice Hall Publishing, 1992, p.91.

VII. Rest and Relaxation

- 📖 Get a **good night's sleep** every night before teaching.

- 📖 Do not drink **caffeine** or **eat heavily** late in the evening if you know it will **disturb** your **sleep**.

- 📖 Try **exercise** if you are having problems sleeping.

- 📖 Try to stay on the **same** arising and retiring **schedule** on **weekends**.

- 📖 Seek the help of a **physician** if you continually are not sleeping well.

- 📖 Read an interesting **book, journal** or **magazine** when retiring.

- 📖 Listen to **music** that relaxes you.

- 📖 Take a warm and restful **bath** in the evening.

- 📖 Treat colleagues and students **fairly** and **settle problems** as soon as possible so that they do not interfere with your rest and relaxation.

- 📖 **Admit** when you are **wrong** and move on to the rest of your life.

I will lay me down in peace, and sleep.

- Psalms 4:8

Night with her train of stars
And her great gift of sleep.

William Ernest Henley
John Bartlett,
Bartlett's Familiar Quotations.
Boston: Little Brown and Company, 1992, p. 557.

VIII. Reward Yourself

- 📖 **Budget money specifically** for **rewarding yourself**.

- 📖 Go to a museum, botanical garden, aquarium, zoo, park, beach, etc. of your choice as an **economical** reward.

- 📖 As often as you can, **telephone** someone **far away** that you miss and talk to them for at least ten minutes.

- 📖 Dress up and go to a **restaurant** you think is elegant and expensive.

- 📖 Lock the door on the bathroom for **fifteen minutes** and sit in a nice warm **bath**.

- 📖 Budget and save to purchase a small portable **spa** and use it regularly.

- 📖 **Indulge** yourself with a **professional massage** from time to time.

- 📖 Budget and save money for **vacations**, weekends or longer.

- 📖 Budget and save money for **purchases** that are really **important** to you and **BUY** them.

- 📖 Take time to **cook, bake, sew, knit, send cards, write letters, etc., for others** which you find rewarding to do.

Noble deeds and hot baths are the best cures for depression.
- Dodie Smith

Stop the habit of wishful thinking and start the habit of thoughtful wishes.
- Mary Martin

It's easier to act your way into new ways of feeling than to feel yourself into new ways of acting.
- Susan Glaser

Carolyn Warner, Treasury of Women's Quotations.
Englewood Cliffs, New Jersey: Prentice Hall Publishing, 1992, pp. 15, 14, 13.

IX.   Mental Exercises

- 📖 **Practice patience** at every conceivable opportunity.

- 📖 **Concentrate** on what you are able to **accomplish,** not what you could not do.

- 📖 **Form** your own **opinions** of **students**, do not elicit or accept preconceived notions of others.

- 📖 Accept that **students earn** their **grades** as opposed to you gave them a grade.

- 📖 Realize that **administrators** and **counselors** are involved with many school programs and practice patience.

- 📖 Set **achievable short** term and **long** term **goals** for yourself and **write** them down. Refer to them often.

- 📖 Twenty minutes of **planning** spent **relaxing** with nothing accomplished is better than an hour of planning spent stressfully.

- 📖 **Change** the things that you can change, **accept** the things that you cannot change, and learn to **recognize** things as one or the other.

- 📖 Learn **yoga** and/or other types of **mental relaxations**.

Always give your best, never get discouraged, never be petty; always remember, others may hate you. Those who hate you don't win unless you hate them. And then you destroy yourself.

- Richard M. Nixon, August 9, 1974.
Daniel B. Baker, *Power Quotes.*
Detroit: Visible Ink Press, 1992, p. 93.

X. Professionalism

- Always **act** like a **professional** when representing your profession.
- **Dress** as a **professional** when representing your profession.
- **Read** and **stay current** about your profession.
- Be an **active** member of **professional organizations**.
- Attend **workshops** and in-**services** with an **open mind** to acquiring information and rejuvenation.
- Learn about **candidates** and **vote** according to what is best for your profession.
- Be **open** to **new ideas** and **innovations** in teaching, much like what you expect from your students.
- **Speak highly** of your **profession** and your **school** to **everyone**.
- **Associate** with those in your profession who are **positive** and **motivated**.
- Be **proud** of your profession!

Those who educate children well are more to be honored than their parents, for these only give them life; those the art of living well.

— Aristotle

P. Susan Mamchak and Steven R. Mamchak,
Educator's Lifetime Library of Stories, Anecdotes, Wit and Humor.
West Nyack, New York: Parker Publishing Company, 1979, p. 244.

<u>Notes</u>

Notes

References and Resources

Books:

📖 Aron, Elaine, *The Highly Sensitive Person: How To Thrive When the World Overwhelms You*. New York: Broadway Books, 1997.

📖 Battison, Toni, *Beating Stress*. New York: Macmillan, 1997.

📖 Cunningham, J. Barton, *The Stress Management Sourcebook*. Los Angeles: Lowell House, Contemporary Books, 1997.

📖 Davis, Martha, Elizabeth Robbins Eshelman, Matthew McKay, *The Relaxation and Stress Reduction Workbook, 4th edition.* Oakland, CA: New Harbinger Publications, 1995.

📖 Eliot, Robert S., *From Stress to Strength: How to Lighten Your Load and Save Your Life*. New York: Bantam Books, 1995.

📖 Eshref, Hussein, *Easy Exercises to Relieve Stress*. Holbrook, MA: Adams Media Corporation, 1999.

📖 George, Mike, *Learn to Relax: A Practical Guide to Easing Tension and Conquering Stress*. San Francisco: Chronicle Books, 1998.

📖 Giacobello, John, *Everything You Need To Know About The Dangers of Overachieving: A Guide for Relieving Pressure and Anxiety*. New York: Rosen Publishing Group, 2000.

📖 Girdano, Daniel A., *Controlling Stress and Tension: A Holistic Approach*. Boston: Allyn and Bacon, 1996.

📖 Gordon, James Samuel, *Stress Management*. Philadelphia, PA: Chelsea House Publishers, 2001

📖 Hargreaves, Gerard, *Stress Management: The Essential Guide to Thinking and Working Smarter*. New York: AMACOM, 1999.

📖 Hawkins, Don, *Overworked: Successfully Managing Stress in the Workplace*. Chicago: Moody Publishing, 1996.

📖 Inlander, Charles B., *Stress: 63 Ways to Relieve Tension and Stay Healthy*. New York: Walker and Company, 1996.

📖 Ladas-Gaskin, Carol, *Instant Stress Relief*. Kansas City: Andrews McMeel Publishing, 1997.

📖 Lark, Susan M., *Dr. Susan Lark's Anxiety and Stress Self-Help Book*. Berkeley, CA: Celestial Arts, 1996.

📖 LaRoche, Loretta, *How Serious is This?: Seeing Humor in Daily Stress*. Plymouth, MA: Lighthearted Productions, 1996.

📖 Lazarus, Judy, *Stress Relief and Relaxation Techniques*. Los Angeles: Keats Publishing, 2000.

📖 Leatz, Christine Ann, *Career Success / Personal Stress: How to Stay Healthy in a High-Stress Environment*. New York: McGraw-Hill, 1993.

📖 Levy, Lois B., *Undress Your Stress: 30 Curiously Fun Ways To Take Off Tension*. Naperville, IL: Sourcebooks, 1999.

📖 Malkin, Mort, *Aerobic Walking*. New York: Wiley, 1995.

📖 Maslach, Christina, *The Truth About Burnout: How Organizations Can Cause Personal Stress and What To Do About It*. San Francisco: Jossey-Bass Publishing, 1997.

📖 Matthews, A. M., *The Seven Keys to Calm: Essential Steps for Staying Calm Under Any Circumstances*. New York: Pocket Books, 1997.

📖 Murray, Michael T., *Stress, Anxiety, and Insomnia: How You Can Benefit from Diet, Vitamins, Minerals, Herbs, Exercise, and Other Natural Methods*. Rocklin, CA: Prima Publishing, 1995.

📖 Nichol, David, *The One-Minute Mediator: Relieving Stress and Finding Meaning in Everyday Life*. Cambridge, MA: Perseus Publishing, 2001.

📖 Null, Gary, *Gary Null's Ultimate Lifetime Diet*. New York: Broadway Books, 1999.Schlosberg, Suzanne, *The Ultimate Workout Log: An Exercise Diary and Fitness Guide*. Boston: Houghton Mifflin Company, 1999.

📖 Powell, Trevor J., *Free Yourself From Harmful Stress*. New York: DK Publishing, 1997.

📖 Seligman, Martin E. P., *Learned Optimism: How to Change Your Mind and Your Life*. New York: Simon and Schuster Trade, 1998.

📖 Turkington, Carol A., *Stress Management For Busy People*. New York: McGraw Hill, 1998.

Journals and Magazines:

📖 **Health and Stress:** American Institute of Stress, 124 Park Ave, Yonkers NY 10703; E-mail: stress124@earthlink.net; Phone: 914-963-1200

📖 More online at **http://www.publist.com**

Internet Sites:

📖 **Excite Health: Mental Health,** search for other stress management sites, http://www.excite.com/health

📖 **Michigan Teacher Network - Health, Fitness, and Life,** resources for stress management, International Stress Management Assn., http://mtn.merit.edu/resources/health

📖 **Mind/Body Medical Institute Website,** relaxation techniques and stress management strategies, http://mindbody.harvard.edu

📖 **NEA Today: Books,** topics such as stress management, time management, etc., http://www.nea/org/neatoday/9905/books

📖 **ProTeacher,** miscellaneous topics including stress management and classroom management, http://www.proteacher.com.

📖 **School Futures -Stress Management for Teachers,** especially for new teachers, http://www.schoolfutures.org/inteastress.html.

📖 **Stress Management Institute,** Ann Sturgis, Ph. D., http://www.deletestress.com.

📖 **Stress Management Training Institute,** http://www.smti.org

📖 **Teacher Voices,** teacher chat room and message board, http://www.teachervoices.com.

📖 **The Yoga Site,** online yoga source center, http://www.yogasite.com

Chapter 8: Know the Essentials of School Law

Over the last half of the twentieth century the American Public School System has become an extremely litigious entity. Superintendents, principals, school board members and teachers have been sued at escalating rates. In addition to being sued, some members of the educational community have been fired due to their inability to accurately and legally understand, interpret and apply the legal basis of education. Most students know of a teacher or teachers who have stepped outside of the law (and survived). However, one abiding principle to bear in mind is once a law is violated it only takes one student to file a complaint and call into question the abused statute. **Negligence, abuse of due process, misuse of corporal punishment and proselytizing a religious belief,** are but a few of the ways in which teachers could find themselves enmeshed in legal quandaries.

A basic concept that all teachers must grasp is that students attending public schools in the United States are present under the jurisdiction of a **compulsory attendance** ordinance. Consequently, a teacher's first action in the classroom and around the school building must always be predicated on the safety of the students. Furthermore, teachers must never violate any of the basic doctrines prescribed in the Bill of Rights within the constitution of the United States (e.g. the establishment clause, right to due process, etc.).

The terminology often utilized is **"in loco parentis,"** in place of the parents. This means that the teacher possesses a portion of the parent's rights, duties, and responsibilities. In recent years, the courts have diluted part of this clause; however, it is always best to act in the best interest of the students, remembering..."*in loco parentis.*"

"If...."

If a child lives with criticism,
He learns to condemn.
If a child lives with hostility,
He learns to fight.
If a child lives with ridicule,
He learns to be shy.
If a child lives with shame,
He learns to fee guilty.
If a child lives with tolerance,
He learns to be patient.
If a child lives with encouragement,
He learns confidence.
If a child lives with praise,
He learns to appreciate.
If a child lives with fairness,
He learns justice.
If a child lives with security,
He learns to have faith.
If a child lives with approval,
He learns to like himself.
If a child lives with acceptance and friendship,
He learns to find love in the world.

Dorothy Law Nolte

I.   Religion and the Schools

FIRST AMENDMENT

Congress shall make no law respecting an establishment of religion, or prohibiting the free exercise thereof; or abridging the freedom of speech, or of the press; or the right of the people peaceably to assemble, and to petition the government for a redress of grievances.

- **Teach about** the religions of the world.... **do not proselytize** one specific religious belief.
- Use the Bible, Torah, Koran or other sacred books as **studies in literature.**
- Wear religious jewelry in a **very discreet manner** (if at all).
- Do not lead your class, team, choir, band, etc. in prayer, **even if it is a non-denominational prayer.**
- Grant students **release time** on religious holidays.
- Do not coerce students to participate in a **secular activity if it violates their religious code** (e.g. dissection of an animal, Halloween celebrations, etc.)
- **Monitor your class** to assure that students are neither mocking someone's beliefs nor forcing beliefs on another student.
- If school policy permits, allow students to have a **minute of silence** before or after lunch to spend in silence as they so desire.

📖 Should a debate ensue regarding religion(s), **remain neutral**, and be certain to keep the discussion issue-oriented as opposed to personal attacks.

📖 Permit students to **"rally around the flag"** before and after school for prayer services. Also, religious groups before and after school may use the school building.

THE LEMON TEST

Religion in the Public Schools

1) **A law or policy (textbook, activity, poem, music, etc.) must have been adopted with a secular purpose.**

2) **Its primary effect must neither advance nor inhibit religion.**

3) **It must not result in excessive entanglement of government and religion.**

(Lemon v. Kurtzman, 1979; Wolman v. Walter, 1977)

II.   Always think "SAFETY FIRST."

- The number one reason teachers are sued and/or fired in the United States is **negligence** (acts or omissions demonstrating a failure to use reasonable care.

- Greet your students at the door and remain with them unless called away and someone watches your class. Failure to be with your class is termed: **nonfeasance** (non-care).

- Assign your students tasks that are reasonable and safe. Do not ask a first grade student to carry a glass fish tank down the hall to the fourth grade classroom, or a senior in high school to climb a twelve foot ladder in order to hand a banner: **malfeasance** (bad care).

- Give your students clear, concise and accurate directions. Always emphasize any safety procedures that would protect their well being. When utilizing any potentially dangerous implement such as a scalpel, Bunsen burner, chemicals, etc., always include safety procedures with your initial lessons to assure the students are knowledgeable about the proper usage: **misfeasance** (wrong care).

- Delineate clear precise plans in your **substitute lesson plan book**. Alert the substitute to any potential problems.

- Individually take and **record attendance daily**. Do not allow a student to perform this function for you.

- **Arrive at all assigned** duty assignments in a **timely fashion** and **remain "on duty"** until the correct time has elapsed.

- **Personally inspect and if necessary warn students** of potentially dangerous or faulty playground equipment.

- 📖 **Do not leave a student who misbehaved unattended in the hallway** (or other open area) as a punishment or cooling off period. Make mutual arrangements with another teacher to allow these students to sit in the back of the classroom to "cool off."
- 📖 Alert all **chaperones** on field trips that they are the legal custodians of the students in their care.

Avoid

<u>Malfeasance</u> (*bad* care)

<u>Misfeasance</u> (*wrong* care)

<u>Nonfeasance</u> (*no* care)

III. Private Activities Versus Teaching Effectiveness

- Discipline yourself to acquire a **good night's rest**. Tired teachers often have short (or no) fuses.

- Eat **balanced meals** to fuel your daily work.

- **Do not abuse alcohol** or any other controlled, dangerous substances....especially on school nights!

- Do not participate in public activities that **the local community may find offensive.**

- **Volunteer** some time at the local library, hospital or nursing home to help support community endeavors.

- **Dress appropriately** being especially mindful of the fact that you are a professional.

- Become a member of a **civic organization** (e.g. Kiwanis, Rotary, Jaycees, etc.)

- Keep all personal disagreements with the administration or other teachers **professional and private.**

- Attend the church, synagogue or temple of your choice, but **do not proselytize your beliefs in school.**

- **Support** the Red Cross Blood Drive, United Appeal or other local charities that directly affect your school's community.

REMINDER:
Comments about the community in which one teaches should always be positive or left unsaid!

IV. Corporal Punishment

- 📖 **Avoid corporal punishment**, even if it is legal where you teach.
- 📖 Where legal, leave the processing of corporal punishment to the administration.
- 📖 Be sure to have a **witness** present if you must administer corporal punishment.
- 📖 Adults should never hit children, but especially, **never hit a student while angry.**
- 📖 Be certain that a **written permission slip** from the parents/ guardians is on file in the office.
- 📖 A **specified instrument** should be utilized. This will usually be ascribed by the administration.
- 📖 A specific **amount of "swats"** should be administered according to the guidelines of the school.
- 📖 **Do not permit other students to watch** or be a part of the witness procedure.
- 📖 Maintain **documentation** of all occurrences of corporal punishment with a very specific accounting of the exact circumstances.
- 📖 **Alert the parents/guardians** to what has taken place prior to the student returning home. Beat the problem home; however, be sure to guard against the possibility of child abuse in the home.

REMEMBER: *Violence begets Violence!*

FOURTEENTH AMENDMENT

...No State shall make or enforce any law which shall abridge the privileges or immunities of citizens of the United States; nor shall any State deprive any person of life, liberty, or property, without due process of law; nor deny to any person within its jurisdiction the equal protection of the laws.

- The Constitution of the United State of America

V. Procedural Due Process

📖 In the event of a serious offense committed by a student, **advanced notification of charges** must be given to the student, and with sufficient advance warning.

📖 The student must be given **advance access to the evidence** held against him, and be guaranteed the services of an impartial **decision maker.**

📖 **The student has a right to counsel,** or another representative, to present the arguments against imposition of penalty.

📖 The student has a right to an **interpreter** for a limited English-proficient or hearing-impaired person.

📖 The student has the right to choose whether the **disciplinary hearing** should be **open or closed**.

📖 The student has the right to **confront and cross-examine the witnesses** the school presents.

📖 The student should be afforded the opportunity to make a **full presentation of his or her side** of the case and to raise the issue whether the particular penalty proposed is appropriate.

📖 The student has the right to have the **hearing limited to the original charges,** and to have any evidence excluded from use at the hearing if the evidence was obtained in violation of the be **Fourth Amendment.**

📖 The student has a right to an **oral/written recording** of hearing.

📖 The student has the right to receive **a written document from the impartial decision maker** who conducted the hearing setting forth the determination on whether the rules infraction occurred and, if so, the nature of the penalty to be imposed.

VI. Academic Freedom

📖 Although implied, **K-12 teachers do not possess the same quality of academic freedom** as do college and university professors. (This is mainly due to the fact that K-12 teachers are working with minors.)

📖 Teach the **subject matter** within your content area. (Mathematics teachers should not be discussing abortion.)

📖 Content should be **developmentally appropriate** for the age/grade level you are teaching. (First grade teachers should not be discussing the deleterious effects of crack cocaine.)

📖 Academic freedom does allow the teacher some latitude in choice of **teaching methodology** to employ.

📖 Academic freedom does not allow the teacher to reduce the quantity or quality of content specified by **state and district curriculum guides**.

📖 Academic freedom allows a teacher to expand the quantity and or quality of content specified by the **state and district curriculum guides,** as long as the initial guidelines for mastery have been met.

📖 Teachers should not engage in **personal counseling** that is not directly related to their subject matter.

📖 Teachers should not encourage **civil disobedience** by students (e.g. sit down strike in cafeteria to protest the food)

📖 Teachers may encourage students in all **legal avenues** to protest the food in the cafeteria. (E.g. meeting with the head of food service, the principal, writing letters, etc.)

📖 **Teachers should not engage in public criticism** of the school official, or discuss private "school business" in public forums.

VII. Tenure

- 📖 In recent years there has been some movement to eliminate tenure from the K-12 sector. (**Georgia** is one state that has successfully abolished tenure for K-12 teachers.)

- 📖 States and school districts will vary in their **requirements** for earning tenure. (process - length of probationary period, etc.)

- 📖 **Non-tenured teachers** may be released from their position at the end of the academic year without a specified reason.

- 📖 During the contract year, non-tenured teachers are protected under the due process statutes of the **fourteenth amendment**.

- 📖 To release a **tenured teacher** from a position at the end of an academic year the administration must be able to establish a justifiable reason for termination. However, this may vary in degree and could be as simple as a statement that the teacher does not fit the mission of the school or school district.

- 📖 Tenure **will not protect** a teacher who has violated a law and been convicted in a court of law. (E.g. grand theft, larceny, child molestation, etc.)

- 📖 In most instances, **when changing school districts**, even within the same state, tenure will need to be re-earned.

- 📖 **State or national board teacher certification** is excellent enhancement for earning tenure but does not guarantee tenure.

- 📖 Unfortunately, **the history of tenure has yielded the protection of BAD teachers**.

- 📖 However, **the history of tenure protects the truly GREAT experimental teachers** who are innovative and risk takers. These risk takers might possibly never attain their greatest accomplishments. In addition, tenure has been a shield protecting teachers from unscrupulous administrator, racists and bigots.

VIII. Search and Seizure

In general, schools **do not need justifiable cause** to conduct a search. They only **need reasonable suspicion.** The rational is that the minors in the building are being compelled to be there by law; consequently, the adults in the building must take all necessary precautions to protect their safety.

Teachers and administrators **may conduct a search under any of the following circumstances**: 1) a student informs a teacher that another student is carrying a concealed weapon. 2) a teacher receives a note indicating that a specific student is carrying a controlled dangerous substance (drugs).   3) the office receives an anonymous phone call stating that a student has brought an explosive to school.

Low risk searches for both teachers and administrators are: open view, school property, school locker, desk, and a student's car when a danger exists (weapon).

Moderate risk searches for both teachers and administrators are: empty purse, empty pockets, and frisk/pat down.

High risk searches for both teachers and administrators are: a student's car when no danger exists, partial disrobe, strip search and body cavity search.

A witness should be present for ALL searches, even low risk.

A K9 Police Dog may not be utilized to randomly search students.

A K9 Police Dog may be utilized to randomly search lockers, book bags or a specific student who has been identified as a potential carrier of a weapon or controlled dangerous substance (drugs).

- **Metal detectors** and other like devices may be utilized to screen for weapons.

- A student who **claims to have a weapon or controlled dangerous substance - DOES!** Even if it is a false brag or a cheap imitation, for all practical purposes it <u>MUST</u> be regarded as the real thing.

<u>SEARCHES OF STUDENTS</u>

The Supreme Court's two-pronged test:

1.) Is the search justified at its inception?

2.) Is the search, when actually conducted, "reasonably related in scope to the circumstances which justified the interference in the first place?"

(New Jersey v. T.L.O. 1985)

IX.   Private Schools and Homeschools

📖 The use of public funds to provide secular services to private schools has led to a concept referred to as the **Child Benefit Theory.**

📖 The Supreme Court reasoned that the use of public funds for **transportation** for students in parochial schools benefited the children and not the school or a religion.

📖 The Supreme Court reasoned that the use of public funds for **textbooks** for students in parochial schools benefited the children and not the school or a religion.

📖 The Supreme Court reasoned that the use of public funds for **some special services** (e.g. speech pathology, hearing impaired, etc.) for students in parochial schools benefited the children and not the school or a religion.

📖 **Education in a child's home** can meet the requirement of compulsory education. (HOMESCHOOLING)

📖 States have individually defined **requirements** for the teachers of homeschoolers.

📖 Home instruction must be **equivalent** to what a school provides. Periodic checks are conducted by state officials.

📖 Home instruction must be carried out **in good faith** and not as a subterfuge to avoid sending children to school.

📖 Homeschoolers **may participate** in some public school specific classes, athletic teams, band, chorus, clubs, etc. However, there are guidelines which cover there actual participation

📖 Homeschoolers must **take and pass all standardized examinations** or be compelled to attend the local public school.

X. Legal Advice for Student Teachers

- 📖 Read the **teachers handbook!** Discuss its contents with the cooperating teacher. Be sure you understand its requirements and prohibitions.

- 📖 Thoroughly discuss school **safety rules and regulations.** Be certain you know what to do in case of an emergency, before assuming complete control of the classroom.

- 📖 Be aware of the **potential hazards** associated with any activity and act accordingly to protect children from those dangers.

- 📖 Be certain you know what **controls the district** has placed on the **curriculum** you will be teaching. Are there **specific tests** and/or **methodologies** that district policy requires or prohibits?

- 📖 Be certain that **student records** are used to enhance and inform your teaching. Make certain that strict confidentiality is respected.

- 📖 **Document any problems** you have with students, or as a teacher, in case you are asked to relate details at a later time.

- 📖 **Dress professionally** at all times. This is especially pertinent for secondary education student teachers, who in some cases may be just a few years older than some of the seniors in the high school.

- 📖 Maintain the **exact same schedule** as the cooperating teacher to which you are assigned. Do not skip out on faculty meetings, parent conferences, etc.

- 📖 **Do not fraternize** with students outside of the school day. This is a potential problem for secondary education student teachers.

- 📖 Be sure that your **medical records** are up to date and that you have all the necessary shots to begin your student teaching.

Notes

Notes

References and Resources

Books:

Brinkley, J. W., *Students' Legal Rights on a Public School Campus*. Fort Worth, TX: Roever Communications, 1993.

Deskbook Encyclopedia of American School Law, 2002. Birmingham, AL: Oakstone Legal and Business Publishing, 2001.

Fireside, Harvey, *The Fifth Amendment: The Right to Remain Silent*. Springfield, NJ: Enslow Publishers, 1998.

Fischer, Louis, *Teachers and the La*w. New York: Longman Publishing, 1991.

Fuller, Sarah Betsy, *Hazelwood v. Kuhlmeier: Censorship in School Newspapers*. Berkeley Height, NJ: Enslow Publishers, 1998.

Hartmeister, Fred, *Surviving as a Teacher: The Legal Dimension*. Chicago: Precept Press, 1995.

Katz, Lewis R., *Know Your Rights*. Cleveland, Ohio: Banks-Baldwin Law Publishing, 1993.

Kirp, David L., *Learning By Heart: AIDS and Schoolchildren in America's Communities*. New Brunswick, NJ: Rutgers University Press, 1989.

Kronenwetter, Michael, *Under 18: Knowing Your Rights*. Hillside, NJ: Enslow Publishers, 1993.

Langford, Duncan, Editor, *Internet Ethics*. New York: St. Martin's Press, 2000.

Legal Basics: A Handbook for Educators. Bloomington, IN: Phi Delta Kappa Educational Foundation, 1998.

McGilbray, Anne, Introduction and Editor, *Governing Childhood*. Brookfield, VT: Dartmouth Publishing, 1997.

📖 *Migrant Education Program Policy Manual: Migrant Education Programs Operated by State Education Agencies*. Washington D.C.: U.S. Department of Education, Office of Migrant Education, 1992.

📖 O'Neil, Robert M., *Classrooms in the Crossfire: the Rights and Interests of Students, Parents, Teachers, Administrators, Librarians, and the Community*. Bloomington, IN: Indiana University Press, 1981.

📖 Ratliff, Stan and Carole Veir, *The Nightmare of Being Sued as a Teacher: Handbook on the Legal Aspects of Education for Teachers and Student Teachers*. Westminster, CO: SEJI Publications, 1984.

📖 Rossow, Lawrence F., *Students and the Law*. Bloomington, IN: Phi Delta Kappa Educational Foundation, 1991.

📖 Sherrow, Victoria, *Censorship in Schools*. Springfield, NJ: Enslow Publishers, 1996.

📖 Stoner, Madeleine R., *The Civil Rights of Homeless People: Law, Social Policy, and Social Work Practice*. New York: Aldine de Gruyter, 1995.

📖 Strickland, Rennard, *Avoiding Malpractice: A Practical Legal Handbook for the Teaching Professional*. New York: Hawthorn Books, 1976.

📖 Turner, Donald G., *Legal Issues in Education of the Handicapped*. Bloomington, IN: Phi Delta Kappa Educational Foundation, 1983.

📖 Wong, Glenn M., *Essentials of Law in Amateur Sports*. Dover, MA: Auburn House Publishing, 1988.

Journals and Magazines:

📖 **Children and the Law:** American Bar Association, 750 N Lake Shore Dr, Chicago IL 60611; Phone: 312-988-5555

📖 **Education Law**: Matthew Bender & Co., Inc, 2 Park Ave, New York NY 10016; E-mail: international@bender.com; Phone: 212-448-2000

📖 **Legal Assistant Today**: James Publishing Inc., P O Box 25202, Santa Ana, CA, 92799-5202; http://www.jamespublishing.com; latsubscriptions@jamespublishing.com; 714-755-5450.

📖 **School Law News**: Aspen Publishers, 7201 McKinney Circle, Frederick MD 21701-9782; E-mail: customer.service@aspenpubl.com; Phone: 301-417-7500

📖 **School Law Reporter**: Education Law Association, 818 Miriam Hall, 300 College Park, Dayton OH 45469-2280; E-mail: ela@udayton.edu; Phone: 937-229-3589

📖 More online at **http://www.publist.com**

Internet Sites:

📖 **Education Law Association**, http://www.educationlaw.org

📖 **Education Week and Teacher Magazine**, http://www.edweek.org

📖 **Eduhound**, educational databases, http://www.eduhound.com

📖 **National Education Association,** http://nea.org

📖 **School Law Bulletin**, http://ncinfo.iog.unc.edu

📖 **United States Department of Education**, http://www.ed.gov

Chapter 9: Parents/Guardians and Administrators

Communication is the essential ingredient in all good teaching. This art should not be limited only to the classroom. For teachers to be successful they MUST know how to communicate with the student's parents/guardians and the school's administration. Teachers across centuries have identified the parents/guardians as the primary educators. Whether it is a child not getting enough rest, or understanding his multiplication tables, or exhibiting unruly behavior, the parents/guardians could prove to be an invaluable source of support to the teacher. However there are two golden rules that need to be followed when eliciting the help of parents/guardians. **First, make contact with the parents/guardians early in the year**. Do not wait for a huge problem to arise. Secondly, **make the first contact as positive as possible.** If possible, plan a positive contact for all your students' parents! Naturally, this is only doable in the elementary grades due to the amount of students an elementary teacher has to work with versus that of a middle or high school teacher. Administrators' primary function is to facilitate the learning environment for the teachers. When communicating with them it is always wise to remember that your problem, which seems the largest in the world, is one of several that administrators are currently trying to work through in order to have the whole school run efficiently.

I.   Parents/Guardians: Contacting

- **Contact parents/guardians early** with an introductory letter at the beginning of the school year or a newsletter. Interns should do this during their first week of internship.

- Contact parents/guardians for **positive reasons** as early in the year as possible.

- Accentuate the positive before dealing with problems at any time during the school year.

- **Date all materials** that you send home to parents whether to individuals or to all parents/guardians. Sending **e-mails** and/or attaching documents automatically provide a **dated reference**.

- **Use plain, everyday language** versus education jargon in communications to parents/guardians. (ESE, ESOL, IEP, etc.)

- Continue throughout the year to contact parents/guardians positively with an **informative letter or newsletter**. Try to have some focus on ALL of your students. You could send electronically attached to e-mail.

- Contact parents/guardians **as soon as possible when a problem** arises to try to eliminate it as soon as possible. Use e-mail or consider even having someone cover your class while you make a phone call if the actions warrant your immediate action.

- Inform parents/guardians **in a timely manner when a student is doing poorly**, especially if he/she is in danger of failing a subject.

- **Create form letter templates** on the computer that can be filled in quickly for a variety of topics to send to parents/guardians.

- Whether you access **e-mail** at your school or at home, solicit e-mail addresses from parents/guardians for quick contacts.

138

II. Parents/Guardians: Documentation

☐ **Make a copy of e-mail or hard copies of correspondence** sent to parents/guardians. (Invest in an inexpensive scanner-copier for your classroom. You can even keep the documentation on disks or hard drive.)

☐ Keep a record of **when and how a communication** was sent such as by student, mail, e-mail, courier pigeon, etc.

☐ **Keep a file of communications** received from parents/guardians.

☐ **Collect data, student's work, student's correspondence, etc.** to share with parents/guardians concerning student's progress.

☐ **Keep a record of phone calls** and what was discussed with a parent/guardian for future reference.

☐ **Keep a copy of letters, newsletters, etc**. that you send home as general correspondence to parents/guardians for future reference.

☐ Keep a record of all **referrals** to the office and action taken.

☐ Ask that **parents/guardians sign certain documents** such as tests, quizzes, projects, etc. and keep a record that these documents were returned to you with the parents'/guardians signatures.

☐ **Keep a record of all efforts** made to help a student who is having problems, such as individual tutoring, peer tutoring, giving student flash cards, etc.

☐ **Make documentation as simple as possible,** perhaps with a spreadsheet or table with columns for phone calls, written communication, e-mail, helping strategies, etc. (that you can label easily with dates, and attach copies of letters, etc.

III. Parents/Guardians: Open Communication

- Be sure to learn the **correct names** and **relationship** to students of the parents/guardians for any communications specifically addressed to them.

- **Invite and welcome parental/guardian communications** from the beginning by sharing your contact information and requesting contact information such as phone, e-mail, etc.

- **Solicit helpful information** from parents/guardians regarding their student, such as allergies, medications, interests, etc.

- **Provide opportunities for parents/guardians (with necessary approval) to come into the classroom** for plays, viewing projects, etc. to build a positive rapport that makes parents/guardians feel welcome.

- Welcome (approved) parents/guardians into the classroom as **volunteers**.

- Invite (approved) parents/guardians into the classroom to share **talents, travels, interests, careers**, etc.

- When problems arise, stress the importance of a ***combined effort*** to help the student.

- In parent/guardian conferences, allow parents/guardians the opportunity to express their opinion and **listen with an open mind.**

- In parent/guardian conferences communicate what you intend to do, **but also solicit from the parents/guardians what they will do** to make this a combined effort before ending the conference.

- Communicate to parents/guardians when a problem is resolved to inform them of **positive results.**

IV. Parents/Guardians: Involvement

📖 Solicit from parents/guardians (with necessary approval) at the beginning of the year **a list of things that they will be willing to help you** with during the school year, perhaps by sending home a checklist to be signed. Don't forget the Dads!

📖 **Provide a mini-workshop** before or after school for (approved) parents/guardians who want to volunteer to **tutor**, etc. in the classroom to set down guidelines and expectations for volunteers.

📖 **Contact (approved) parents/guardians with specific dates, times, and purposes** when utilizing their help for tutoring, demonstrations, etc.

📖 Encourage parents/guardians early in the year to join and support the school's **Parent-Teacher Organization**, etc. and lead by your example.

📖 Invite (approved) parents/guardians who are **knowledgeable in computers** or who are willing to help students select library books, etc. to come in during those scheduled times during the week to help students.

📖 Solicit the help of (approved) parents/guardians **who are available to help with morning** lunch count (not attendance), oral reading, etc. to free you up for individual or small group tutoring in the morning.

📖 Invite (approved) parents/guardians to assist on **field trips** and such **fun events,** preferably those who have been helpful in other capacities.

📖 Remember to **communicate the need for assistance** when parents/guardians are on site or through newsletters, etc.

📖 **Recognize parents/guardians for their help** by such things as monthly certificates or a section of the class newsletter, etc.

V.   Parents/Guardians: Difficult Communications

□ If parents/guardians are hostile one the phone, **excuse yourself and tell them that you will call back** at another more convenient time.

□ If a parent/guardian sends you hostile mail or e-mail, especially threatening mail, **inform the principal and counselors** and keep the letter on file.

□ If a parent/guardian enters the classroom in a hostile or threatening manner, **try to step outside the classroom** with them and ask them to meet you at the office, because you cannot leave your class now. Hopefully you can call the office.

□ If a parent/guardian enters the classroom in a hostile or threatening manner and will not step outside the classroom, **ask the students to go to the principal's office or another teacher's classroom.** Ask one of them to get the principal to come immediately to your classroom.

□ If a parent/guardian comes to a conference in a hostile manner, **have a tape recorder handy** and ask the parent if you may tape record the conference.

□ If a parent/guardian who is hostile does not want you to tape record the conference, begin **writing down everything** you can possibly remember that they say and tell them that is what you are doing. (Use a large yellow legal pad.)

□ **Protect your students and yourself at all times** and act accordingly. Have a plan of action with other teachers near your classroom.

□ When the parent/guardian is **calm**, resume the conference with another colleague or administrator present.

VI. Administration: Observe School Rules and Procedures

☐ **Obtain** and **study** so that you know the **faculty handbook**.

☐ If there is no faculty handbook, **consider helping to get one organized** because everyone will appreciate one.

☐ Know district/school **policy** and district/school **rules** that encompass all classrooms.

☐ Know **procedures** for setting up field trips, ordering supplies, calling in sick, requesting personal leave days, etc.

☐ Plan **activities** to celebrate holidays, birthdays, etc. that respect the district's/school's guidelines.

☐ Observe **school guidelines** for attending schoolwide assemblies, communicate these expectations to the students, and enforce these rules

☐ At the beginning of the year, know specifics regarding **fire drills and tornado drills**, communicate these expectations to the students, and enforce these rules during fire/tornado drills

☐ Know and utilize **procedures for referring students** to the office (discipline), counselors (personal problems, behavior problems, etc), reading specialists (reading difficulty), etc.

☐ Know how to construct an **Individualized Education Plan** and be prepared to do so for each of your students.

☐ Model support for district/school rules and procedures in the **community** and in the **classroom**.

VII. Administration: Follow Professional Guidelines

📖 **Dress according** to the district's/school's dress code for faculty.

📖 Keep all disagreements with administrators on a **professional level;** avoid taking it outside of the school environment.

📖 **Make positive comments** to the community about your school and reserve criticisms for personal and appropriate avenues within the school.

📖 Limit comments about students and parents/guardians to **positive** statements when out in the community.

📖 Make only **factual statements** about happenings at the school to the community.

📖 Limit comments about other faculty to **positive statements** when out in the community.

📖 Restrict days away from your profession to **illness and the allotted personal days**.

📖 **Be proud of the district** and school for which you teach and make that evident by supporting all programs.

📖 **Restrict the time that you spend in the faculty lounge** when negative discussion is the precedent.

📖 **Share positive events**, accomplishments, awards, etc. with the local media to promote the district/school.

Einstein was a man who could ask immensely simple questions.

- Jacob Bronowski

VIII. Administration: Punctuality

- Make a habit of being at school at the time requested by your administration. **(ON TIME)**
- Be responsible enough to **call** and **inform** your administrator when you must arrive later then the requested time.
- **Attend** faculty meetings, parent-teacher organization meetings, back-to-school nights, **and all meetings that require your presence on time.**
- **Complete reports, inventories, etc. in a timely manner.**
- **Begin instruction at the assigned time** to account for all the time allotted for instruction.
- **Send students to their next class,** (including their physical education class, music class, art class, etc.) at the appropriate time.
- **Remain on campus** until the dismissal time for teachers and utilize the time wisely.
- When you must leave early, **inform your administration** so that they are aware of your absence.
- Expect your **administrators to be punctual** also!
- **Model punctuality for your students** on an every day basis.

"Unfaithfulness in the keeping of an appointment is an act of clear dishonesty. You may as well borrow a person's money as his time."
- Horace Mann, political activist for education

"If I have made an appointment with you, I owe you punctuality, I have no right to throw away your time, if I do my own"
- Richard Cecil, clergyman

IX.   Administration: Mutual Support

- 📖 Analyze the importance of a problem or situation. Handle problems that do not need administrative attention and avoid overdoing requests for their assistance. **Solicit the help of your administrator with difficult problems**, situations, etc.

- 📖 Make it known to your administration that you are **supportive of their efforts** and **willing to help** when necessary.

- 📖 **Praise your administration** to parents and others in the community for accomplishments and innovations that you support.

- 📖 **Write** to both **your principal** and **your superintendent** when you feel that your administrator is deserving of praise.

- 📖 **Invite** the **administration** to **visit your classroom** for plays, displays of student work, and other positive gatherings.

- 📖 **Let students know that you support the administration** and discuss the reasons for rules, procedures, etc. that are necessary to run a school safely and efficiently early in the school year.

- 📖 **Respectfully disagree with decisions** and intellectually discuss your opinion with your administrator.

- 📖 **Keep disagreements professional** and never make them public to the community.

- 📖 **Openly discuss ideas** and make suggestions to your administration and be willing to listen to their input.

- 📖 Look for the **positive** and expect the best from your administration.

X. Administration: Expectations

- 📖 Discuss with your **administrator his/her expectations** for your classroom, faculty meetings, etc.

- 📖 Respectfully discuss your **expectations of your administrators** with them.

- 📖 **Address a problem immediately** to avoid allowing it to fester and grow out of proportion.

- 📖 **Discuss problems** with an administrator before going elsewhere for a solution.

- 📖 **Write down what you believe are fair** expectations and discuss them with your administrator.

- 📖 **Ask for clarification** and reasons for changes of assignments, room changes, etc.

- 📖 Try to be **flexible** and accepting of change, which is an ever-constant component of teaching.

- 📖 Let your administration know **when you do not have the materials**, etc. to accomplish their goals.

- 📖 Keep a **sense of humor** and hope that your administrator will too.

- 📖 Do not ask of your administrator what you are not willing to do yourself. **Examine your administration in your classroom.**

"High achievement always takes place in the framework of high expectation."
- Charles Kettering, engineer, inventor

"The quality of expectations determines the quality of our action.
- A. Godin, French writer
- (http://en.thinkexist.com/quotes/a._godin/)

<u>Notes</u>

<u>Notes</u>

References and Resources

Books:

📖 Barth, Roland S., *Improving Schools From Within: Teachers, Parents, and Principals Can Make the Difference*. San Francisco: Jossey-Bass, 1990.

📖 Benjamin, Arthur, *Teach Your Child Math: Making Math Fun For Both of You*. Los Angeles: Lowell House, Contemporary Books, 1996.

📖 Bernard, Michael Edwin, *You Can Do It!: How To Boost Your Child's Achievement in School*. New York: Warner Books, 1997.

📖 Calkins, Lucy McCormick, *Raising Lifelong Learners: A Parent's Guide*. Reading, MA: Addison-Wesley Publishing, 1997.

📖 Dargatz, Jan Lynette, *Simple Truths*. Nashville,TN: T. Nelson Publishers, 1995.

📖 Green, Gordon W., *Helping Your Child To Learn*. Secaucus, NJ: Carol Publishing Group, 1994.

📖 Green, Nancy Sokol, *Raising Curious Kids*. New York: Crown Trade Paperbacks, 1995.

📖 *Home Environment and School Learning: Promoting Parental Involvement in the Education of Children*. San Francisco: Jossey-Bass, 1993.

📖 Jones, Linda T., *Strategies for Involving Parents in Their Children's Education*. Bloomington, IN: Phi Delta Kappa Educational Foundation, 1991.

📖 Lawler, S. Diane, *Parent-Teacher Conferencing in Early Childhood Education*. Washington D.C.: NEA Professional Library, 1991.

📖 Litton, Nancy, *Getting Your Math Message Out To Parents*. Sausalito, CA: Math Solutions Publications, 1998.

📖 Long, Frankie, *Summer Bridge Middle School: 6th to 7th Grade*. Salt Lake City, Utah: Rainbow Bridge Publishing, 1998.

📖 Marshall, Marvin, *Discipline Without Stress Punishments or Rewards: How Teachers and Parents Promote Responsibility and Learning*. Los Alamitos, CA: Piper Press, 2001.

📖 Martz, Larry, *Making School Better: How Parents and Teachers Across the Country are Taking Action*. New York: Time Books, 1992.

📖 McCaleb, Sudia Paolma, *Building Communities of Learners: A Collaboration Among Teachers, Students, Families, and Community*. New York: St. Martin's Press, 1994.

📖 Nolan, Amy, *Great Explorations*. New York: Pocket Books, 1997.

📖 Peters, Ruth Allen, *Overcoming Underachieving: A Simple Plan to Boost Your Kids' Grades and End the Homework Hassles*. New York: Broadway Books, 2000.Popkin, Michael, *Helping Your Child Succeed in School: A Guide for Parents of 4 to 14 Year Olds*. Atlanta, GA: Active Parenting Publications, 1995.

📖 Russell, William F., *Family Learning: How to Help Your Children Succeed in School by Learning at Home*. St. Charles, IL: First World Learning Systems, 1997.

📖 Ryan, Bernard, *Helping Your Child Start School: A Practical Guide for Parents*. Secaucus, NJ: Carol Publishing, 1996.

📖 Stipek, Deborah J., *Motivated Minds: Raising Children to Love Learning*. New York: H. Holt and Company, 2001.

📖 Wiener, Harvey S., *Any Child Can Write*. New York: Oxford University Press, 1994.

📖 Willis, Mariaemma, *Discover Your Child's Learning Style*. Rocklin, CA: Prima Publishing, 1999.

Journals and Magazines:

📖 **American Journal of Education**: University of Chicago Press, 5801 S Ellis Ave., Chicago IL 60637

📖 **Education**: Project Innovation, PO Box 566, Chula Vista CA 92010

📖 **Educational Leadership**: Association for Supervision and Curriculum Development, 125 N West Street, Alexandria VA 22314-2798

📖 **Instructor**: The Instructor Publications, Inc., 7 Bank Street, Dansville NY 14437

📖 **Journal of Educational Psychology**: The American Psychological Association, Inc., 1400 North Uhle Street, Arlington, VA 22201

📖 **Journal of Family Issues**: Sage Publications, 2111 West Hillcrest Drive, Newbury Park CA 91320

📖 **Journal of Research in Childhood Education**: Association for Childhood Education International, 1141 Georgia Ave, Suite 200, Wheaton MD 20902

📖 **Learning Magazine**: PO box 54293, Boulder CO 80322-4293

📖 **National Association of Secondary School Principal's Bulletin**: 1904 Association Drive, Reston, VA 22091

📖 **Parents Magazine**: PO Box 3042, Harlan IA 51593-4207

📖 **School and Community**: Missouri State Teachers Association, PO Box 458, Columbia MO 65205-0458

📖 **School**: Social Issues Resources Series, Inc., PO Box 2507, Boca Raton FL 33432

📖 More online at **http://www.publist.com**

Internet Sites:

📖 **A to Z Kids Stuff Home Page**, http://www.atozkidsstuff.com

📖 **A to Z Teacher Tips: Parent Involvement**, http://www.atozteacherstuff.com

📖 **American Association of School Administrators**, http://aasa.org

📖 **CyberParent**, education topics, http://thecyberparent.com

📖 **Education World**, search topic, http://www.education-world.com

📖 **Family Education**, http://www.familyeducation.com

📖 **Guidance Online**, http://home.cfl.rr.com/nwunder/guidance.html

📖 **Healthy Place**, search the topic, http://www.healthyplace.com

📖 **Inspiring Teachers**, search the topic of parent and teacher relationships, http://www.inspiringteachers.com

📖 **Kids Can Learn**, http://www.kidscanlearn.com

📖 **National Education Association**, http://www.nea.org

📖 **National PTA**, http://www.pta.org/index.stm

📖 **National School Boards Association**, http://www.nsba.org

📖 **Parent Soup Education Central**, parent-teacher conferences, http://www.parentsoup.com/edcentral/stuff/conference.html

📖 **TeachNet**, search the topic, http://teachnet.org

Chapter 10: Utilizing Technology

Technology should be viewed as an **excellent tool** in the classroom. The teacher's use of the tool, no matter what that tool may be, is the key as to whether it will enhance teaching or not. Just as it is up to teachers to make the textbook meaningful to the students, so must the teacher make the computer software meaningful to the students. There is a temptation to think of computer software, because of the visual appeal as well as auditory stimulation, as something that can "stand alone" as a teaching tool. **A computer software program is not a substitute for a caring, analyzing, synthesizing, interacting, thought processing, reflective teacher.** Also, the use of technology in the classroom should not be restricted to the use of the computer in order to provide a true multimedia experience for students.

Technology definitely has its place as an administrative tool that teachers should be taking advantage of on a daily basis. There are multitudes of record keeping tasks that can be simplified and enhanced by the use of the computer. If at all possible, the computer a teacher uses in the classroom should be compatible with the computer used at home so that disks used in the classroom my also be used at home and vice versa.

Teachers who examine software to use in their classrooms and the Internet have found that they may also simulate experiences in the classroom that they could never provide in reality. Teachers need to realize, however, that with the use of the **Internet** comes a responsibility to protect their students from accessing unsuitable information that is also available on-line.

I. Computer-Assisted Instruction

📖 Employ software to **pretest** a particular concept.

📖 As a **supplement** to your teaching, search out tutoring software that **assists** in teaching a specific concept.

📖 Engage students in **constructive practice** of a specific concept through software.

📖 Be sure that tutorial software offers **information** and **tutors** the student when **mistakes** are made.

📖 **Evaluation** is so important in light of standardized tests, so request software that **tests** and **analyzes** students **after** learning the concept.

📖 **Individualize instruction** for the **advanced** student or the student who has been **absent** or **does not grasp** a concept you have taught by letting them work with tutorial software.

📖 Set aside **time** on a **rotating basis** for **all students** to have an opportunity to use the tutorial.

📖 **Introduce** new concepts to the **whole class** with tutorial programs using an **LCD** or **projector**.

📖 Make tutorial software readily available **before** school or **after** school, or even perhaps during **recess** or **lunch**.

📖 Give **students** with **advanced computer skills** opportunities to assist others in using the tutorial software programs.

II. Word Processing

📖 Teach **students** to use word processing to write poems, stories, etc.

📖 **Type** and **duplicate letters** home to **parents/guardians**.

📖 Create or find a **newsletter template** and type in new information **weekly, monthly,** or **periodically** to send **home** with students.

📖 **Type** and **duplicate classroom rules** to give **students** and send one home to **parents**.

📖 Use **text** and **graphics** to create **personalized forms** to send **home** with good news and bad news that can be **checked** or **words filled** in as necessary.

📖 Type **worksheets** and/or **quizzes/tests** that **reflect** specifically what you have **taught**.

📖 Type **administrative tasks** you do at various times during the year and **save** on **disks** to be used when the task comes up again.

📖 Type or **purchase Individual Education Plan** templates that can be easily adjusted for individual students.

📖 Type **directions** for **activities, groupwork,** homework, seatwork, **projects**, etc.

📖 **Fine tune typing skills** with **practice** utilizing such programs as Mavis Beacon Teaches Typing, Mario Teaches Typing, or any such practice software.

📖 Type a **grant** to help acquire technology or any other desirable teaching tool for **your classroom.**

III. Databases

☐ **Collect** important **information** about **students** (name, address, telephone, parents'/guardians' names, birthday, medical data, reading level, etc.) and enter into a database for **organization**.

☐ **Collect** important **information** about **colleagues** (name, address, telephone, birthday, etc.) and enter into a database for **organization**.

☐ Select **birthday** information and run a report for **each month** for both **students** and **colleagues** to help remember their special days throughout the year.

☐ Enter **information collected** by **students** into a database and show them how to **organize** the information.

☐ Create databases of **information** concerning a **particular unit** or **lesson** and **ask** your **students** to search out information using the database(s).

☐ Create a database of **teaching resources** as well as **human resources** so that you can locate the information easily each year.

☐ Create a database for **students** to enter information throughout the school year. For example, create fields for titles, authors, main characters, brief summary, etc. from **student** book **reports**.

☐ **Combine** word processing and database to send **quickly** produced **personalized** letters home at grading time, etc.

☐ Let **students** with **advanced computer skills** assist others in using the database.

☐ Protect **sensitive information** with **passwords** or other security measures.

IV. Spreadsheets

📖 Prepare a **gradebook** with spreadsheet or purchase such a program if the school or district does not provide one.

📖 Prepare an **attendance spreadsheet** or purchase such a program.

📖 Prepare a **budget** for any **purchase allotment** given you for your classroom.

📖 Augment **science** lessons that include **formulas** by using the formulas in **spreadsheets**.

📖 Enter **student**-collected information from **surveys** of students, family, etc. into spreadsheets to **analyze** as percents, etc.

📖 **Analyze** information gathered from **scientific experiments** with spreadsheets.

📖 Prepare **grant request budgets** with a spreadsheet.

📖 Teach **students** to enter **numbers** and **formulas** into a spreadsheet and select information to make **charts**.

📖 Let **students** with **advanced computer skills** assist others in using the spreadsheet.

📖 Complete **administrative tasks** such as **inventories** with the spreadsheet.

> I hear and I forget.
> I see and I remember.
> I do and I understand.
> Ancient Chinese proverb

V. The Internet and Webquests

📖 **Protect** students from **irresponsible information** with software **filters**, **blocks**, **supervision**, etc.

📖 **Warn students against** giving **personal information** about **themselves, family, friends,** etc. on the **Internet.**

📖 **Initially** undertake a **class project** to teach students to use Internet resources.

📖 Direct students to **narrow searches** by using **key words** to find information. Teach students to recognize **irrelevant information** and to use techniques for **scanning**.

📖 **Guide** students to **cite** Internet **sources** correctly.

📖 Locate **existing webquests** or consider **preparing** a **webquest** that compliments a unit, provides cooperative learning opportunities, and is interactive for students.

📖 Arrange a rotating **schedule** that enables **all students** to use Internet resources if you have limited access to computers.

📖 Plan to **schedule opportunities** in a **lab** or the **media center** if the Internet is not available in your classroom.

📖 Let **students with advanced technology skills assist other** students with the **Internet**.

📖 **Graduate** gradually to student developed **webquests** and **group projects** to **reinforce** using Internet resources.

> Knowledge is of two kinds. We know a subject ourselves, or we know where we can find information.   -Samuel Johnson

Bartlett's Familiar Quotations, 16th ed.
Boston: Little, Brown and Company, 1992, pg.316.

VI.   Presentations:(PowerPoint, Corel, ClarisWorks)

📖 Use **templates** to quickly create exciting **personalized multimedia** lessons.

📖 **Convert overhead** projector **lessons** to **multimedia lessons**.

📖 Scan **pictures** (remember **photos** you took during **travels**, etc.), **download** Internet pictures, capture **video**, etc. into **multimedia** lessons for **visual effect**.

📖 Set a **good example** and always **cite sources** of information, pictures, video, etc

📖 Create a multimedia presentation of your classroom to share on **back to school nights**, etc.

📖 Guide a **class project** to create a multimedia presentation providing an opportunity for **everyone** to **contribute**.

📖 Assign **group projects** creating multimedia presentations to **present findings**.

📖 Encourage **students** to create **individual** multimedia presentations to **share** information.

📖 **Share information** with **colleagues** through multimedia presentations on **requested topics**.

📖 Permit **students** with **advanced technology skills** to **assist** others with **multimedia presentations**.

"Man is still the most extraordinary computer of all."
-John F. Kennedy, speech, 1963

Webster's Dictionary of Quotations.

New York: *SMITHMARK Publishers*, 1992, pg. 69

VII. Software Evaluation

📖 **Always evaluate** software **before** you purchase. Utilize **unbiased** software evaluations in journals, magazines or online sources to help you select excellent software for your classroom.

📖 Select software that is **compatible** with the **computers** or **network** on which the software will be loaded. Check with the **technology committee** of your school if uncertain.

📖 Look for clear and precise **directions** that students will find easy to follow.

📖 Examine software for **ease of use.**

📖 Evaluate the software for **fair representation** of all groups, male and female roles, different family situations, etc. Avoid stereotypes.

📖 Be sure that students can work at a **variety of levels**, beginning with easier and advancing to more difficult.

📖 Examine the software for a **variety of activities** to keep students interested in returning to the activities.

📖 Be sure to select software that is **appropriate** for the students' **ages** and **abilities**.

📖 Select software that will let the students **choose their level** and let them **exit** when they are ready.

📖 Choose software that will give you **feedback** concerning students' activities and achievement.

📖 Select software that **enhances** and **strengthens** your curriculum's goals and objectives. .

VIII. Video Recording and Cassette Recording

- 📖 Solicit the **permission** of **parents/guardians** to do video and cassette recording of your students.

- 📖 Allow **rehearsal** or **practice** time **before** any type of videotaping or cassette recording of students.

- 📖 Plan **activities** that lend themselves to **videotaping**, such as, plays, debates, oral reports, talent shows, choral readings, etc.

- 📖 Find **materials** that lend themselves to **cassette recording**, such as, **plays** with **sound effects** or add sound effects to plays that have none and tape record **students** reading.

- 📖 Communicate **expectations** of **acceptable viewing** and **listening behavior prior** to viewing or listening to **recordings** of **students**.

- 📖 Encourage viewing of recordings as **learning experiences** and **opportunities** to grow as a person.

- 📖 Guide students to do activities throughout the **curriculum** and **subject matter** that lend themselves to videotaping or cassette recording, such as original poems, oral reports, etc.

- 📖 Invite **parents/guardians** to attend viewings of videotaped plays, debates, oral reports, etc.

- 📖 **Nurture participation** but **respect** the **rights** of **students** to **decline**.

- 📖 The **teacher** should do the **videotaping** if at all possible to **insure quality** of taping.

IX.   Television, Videos, DVDs, Videodiscs

📖 **Learn** about and **respect copyright laws**. Also, be aware of **school** or **state requirements** concerning videos, DVD's, etc.

📖 Always **preview completely** any program you have **videotaped** to share with students. Never show anything that you have not reviewed.

📖 Discuss **expectations** when viewing television and **model** the expected **behavior** (don't grade papers during the viewing).

📖 Be sure to **relate** to **students** the television program to your **course objectives**.

📖 Plan **follow-up discussion** and/or **activities**.

📖 **Contact** the educational television **network** when using a **particular program** and **acquire** any **materials, suggested objectives,** and/or **activities** to share with students.

📖 Have **students develop** questions as they view a program that they will ask their classmates **following** the **program**.

📖 View **two different** movies or television programs and have the students **analyze** the **similarities** and **differences** (**PLAN AHEAD!**).

📖 Ask students to do **critical analysis** of a story, what **problems** did they find with a **plot**, what **alternative endings** would they suggest, etc.

📖 Span the **subjects** with **historical** programs, **scientist** biographies, **cultural** exploration, etc.

📖 Once in a while allow **students** to **select** a **program** to view for a **reward** for hard work (within your **parameters** and _**NOT**_ **without reviewing first**).

X. Educational Computer Games

📖 **Learn** about and **respect copyright laws** for **software** also.

📖 **Preview** before permitting **students** to play computer games.

📖 **Select** computer games that provide **practice** with a particular **skill.**

📖 Pick computer games that allow students to choose an **easier** or **more difficult** playing **level.**

📖 Elect to use software games that allow students to **end** a session when desired and/or **move** to a **different** part of the game.

📖 Opt for software games that provide a **variety** of ways to present materials.

📖 Choose software games that **vary** the **material** (not repeat the same over and over).

📖 Provide **opportunities** for **all students** to engage in software games.

📖 **Reward** students with software learning games for various reasons.

📖 Let **students** with **advanced technology skills assist** others in using **computer games.**

📖 Put a **portion** of computer game software in storage and bring out those put in storage earlier to **avoid boredom** with repetitive use of the same software.

"It should be noted that the games of children are not games, and must be considered as their most serious actions."

Michel De Montaigne, Essays Webster's Dictionary of Quotations.
New York: SMITHMARK Publishers, 1992, pg. 161.

<u>Notes</u>

<u>Notes</u>

References and Resources

Books:

📖 Brownell, Gregg, *Computers and Teaching.* St. Paul: West Publishing Company, 1992.

📖 Cafolla, Ralph, Dan Kauffman, and Richard Knee, *World Wide Web for Teachers: An Interactive Guide.* Boston: Allyn and Bacon, 1997.

📖 Cannings, Terence R., *The Technology Age Classroom.* Wilsonville, OR: Franklin, Beedle & Associates, 1993.

📖 Dublin, Peter, *Middle and Secondary Math.* New York: Harper Collins College Publishers, 1994.

📖 Ellsworth, Jill H., *Education on the Internet.* Indianapolis, IN: SAMS Publishing, 1994.

📖 Forcier, Richard C., *The Computer As a Productivity Tool in Education.* Englewood Cliffs, NJ: Merrill Publishing, 1996.

📖 Foshay, John D., *Project-Based Multimedia Instruction.* Bloomington, IN: Phi Delta Kappa Educational Foundation, 1999.

📖 Geisert, Paul, Teachers, *Computers and Curriculum: Microcomputers in the Classroom.* Boston: Allyn and Bacon, 1995.

📖 Gibbons, Andrew S., *Computer-Based Instruction: Design and Development.* Englewood Cliffs, NJ: Educational Technology Publications, 1998.

📖 Gimotty, Susan L., *Computer Activities Through the Year.* Westminster, CA: Teacher Created Materials, 1999.

📖 Grabe, Mark, *Integrating Technology for Meaningful Learning.* Boston: Houghton Mifflin Company, 1998.

📖 Grabe, Mark, *Learning With Internet Tools: A Primer.* Boston: Houghton Mifflin Company, 1998.

📖 Harrison, Nigel, *How to Design Self-Directed and Distance Learning.* New York: McGraw Hill, 1999.

📖 Hirschbuhl, John J., editor, *Computer Studies: Computers in Education*. Guilford, Conn: Dushkin Publishing Group, 1994.

📖 Jonassen, David H., Computers in the Classroom: Mindtools for Critical Thinking. Englewood Cliffs, NJ: Merrill Publishing, 1996.

📖 Kearsley, Greg, *Online Education: Learning and Teaching in Cyberspace*. Belmont, California: Wadsworth/Thomson Learning, 2000.

📖 Kehoe, Brendan P and Victoria Mixon, *Children and the Internet: A Zen Guide for Parents and Educators*. Upper Saddle River, New Jersey, 1997.

📖 Khan, Badrul H., editor, *Web-Based Instruction*. Englewood Cliffs, NJ: Educational Technology Publications, 1997.

📖 Leshin, Cynthia B. *Internet Adventures, Version 1.2: Step -By-Step Guide to Finding and Using Educational Resources*. Boston: Allyn and Bacon, 1996.

📖 Lockard, James, Peter D. Abrams, and Wesley A. Many, *Microcomputers for Twenty-First Century Educators, 4th edition*. New York: Longman, 1997.

📖 Maddux, Cleborne D., D. LaMont Johnson, and Jerry W. Willis, *Educational Computing: Learning with Tomorrow's Technologies, 2nd edition*. Boston: Allyn and Bacon, 1997.

📖 McConnell, David, *Implementing Computer Supported Cooperative Learning*. London, Kogan Page, 2000.

📖 McFadden, Charles and Robert E. Yager, project directors, *Scienceplus: Technology and Society*. Austin: Holt, Rinehart & Winston: Harcourt Brace and Jovanovich, 1993.

📖 Merrill, Paul F, Kathy Hammons, Bret R. Vincent, Peter L. Reynolds, Larry Christensen and Marvin N. Tolman, *Computers in Education, 3rd edition*. Boston: Allyn and Bacon, 1996.

📖 Moursund, David, *Increasing Your Expertise as a Problem Solver*. Eugene, OR: International Society for Technology in Education, 1996.

📖 Palloff, Rena M., *Lessons from the Cyberspace Classroom: The Realities of Online Teaching*. San Francisco: Jossey-Bass, 2001.Papert, Seymour, *Mindstorms: Children, Computers, and Powerful Ideas*. New York: Basic Books, 1993.

📖 Perkins, David N., editor, *Software Goes To School: Teaching for Understanding With New Technologies*. New York: Oxford University Press, 1995.

📖 Poole, Bernard John, *Education for an Information Age: Teaching in the Computerized Classroom*. Boston: WCB/McGraw Hill, 1997.

📖 Rittenhouse, Bob and David Spillers, *The Electronic Classroom: Using Technology to Create a 21st Century Curriculum*. Tucson, AZ: Danhouse Publications, Inc, 2000.

📖 Robinette, Michelle, *Windows 95 for Teachers*. Foster City, CA: IDG Books Worldwide, 1997.

📖 Schrum, Lynne and Boris Berenfeld, *Teaching and Learning in the Information Age: A Guide to Educational Telecommunications*. Boston: Allyn and Bacon, 1997.

📖 Stevenson, Nancy. *Office 97*. Foster City, CA: IDG Books Worldwide, 1998.

📖 Tickle, Les, editor, *Design and Technology in Primary School Classroom: Developing Teachers' Perspectives and Practices*. London: Falmer, 1990.

📖 Tiffin, John, *In Search of the Virtual Class: Education in an Information Society*. London, Routlege Publishing, 1995.

📖 Toliver, Pamela R., PCs for Teachers. Foster City, CA: IDG Books Wordwide, 1997.

Journals and Magazines:

📖 **Cable in the Classroom:** Connell Communications, Inc., 86 Elm St, Peterborough, NH 03458; Phone: 800-216-2225

📖 **Computerworld**: 500 Old Connecticut Path, PO Box 9171, Framingham, MA 01701-9171

📖 **Educational Technology Research and Development**: Association for Educational Communications and Technology, 1126 16th Street NW, Washington, DC 20036

📖 **Information Today**: Learned Information, Inc., 143 Old Marlton Pike, Medford NJ 08055

📖 **Information Week**: CMP Publications, Manhasset NY

📖 **Journal of Special Education Technology**: Joseph J. Stowitchek, box 328, George Peabody College, Nashville TN 37203

📖 **Knowledge Quest: Journal of the American Association of School Librarians**: American Library Association, 50 E Huron Street, Chicago IL 60611-2795

📖 **Learning and Leading With Technology**: International Society for Technology in Education, 1787 Agate Street, Eugene OR 97403-1923

📖 **Media and Methods**: American Society of Educators, 1511 Walnut Street, Philadelphia PA 19102

📖 **Technology and Learning**: Miller Freeman, Inc; 600 Harrison St, San Francisco, CA; Homepage: http://www.techlearning.com; Phone: 415-905-2200

📖 **THE Journal**: Ed/Warnshuis Ltd; 150 El Camino Real, Ste 112, Tustin, CA 92780; **E-mail**: cedwards@thejournal.com; charp@eniac.seas.upenn.edu; **Phone**: 714-730-4011

📖 More online at **http://www.publist.com**

Internet Sites:

- **4 Teachers**, teacher technology resource, http://www.4teachers.org
- **Classroom Connect**, http://www.classroom.com
- **Classroom Exchange - ePals**, http://www.epals.com
- **Digital Education Network**, http://www.actden.com
- **Free Worksheets**, http://www.freeworksheets.com
- **GOTSchool Teachers**, http://teachers.gotschool.com
- **International Society for Technology in Education**, http://www.iste.org
- **Lesson Plan Search**, lessonplansearch.com
- **Marco Polo**, no cost Internet training for K-12 teachers, http://marcopolo.worlcom.com
- **Museum Stuff**, http://www.museumstuff.com
- **NASA Quest**, http://quest.arc.nasa.gov
- **Productivity Recipes for Teachers Using Technology**, http://faculty.harker.org/ms/scottc/teachers/recipe.html
- **Scholastic - Teacher's Homepage**, http://teacher.scholastic.com/index.htm
- **School Grants**, http://www.schoolgrants.org
- **The Global Schoolhouse**, http://www.gsh.org
- **Travel the 50 States in Postcards**, http://www.postcardsfrom.com
- **Virtual Field Trips Site**, http://www.field-guides.com
- **Virtual Zoo**, http://library.thinkquest.org/11922

Chapter 11: Meeting the Needs of Diverse Students

In 1975 President Gerald Ford signed into law <u>PL 94-142</u>. This law mandated that the American Public School System **provide an equal opportunity** for all children to obtain an education. Prior to this act special needs children were usually taught in segregated schools out of the **mainstream** education. Naturally, bringing these children into the schools created somewhat of a disturbance, however, teachers began retooling and applying their skills, making every attempt to reach these new students. At the same time, teachers continued on with the accelerated process for their "regular" students. However, the old tools were not enough and the new techniques could not come fast enough. **We have observed the number of students identified as needing extra help due to a disability grow exponentially over the past three decades**. Consequently, the field of Special Education has become the number one recruited position in the field of education. Some education specialists are even calling for every teacher to be a special education teacher. This chapter will introduce a variety of ways to deal with children needing special assistance. **This will also include those students who are not specifically identified as special education students, but nonetheless, having special needs. A few of these would be: the abused child; suicidal student, invisible student, spoiled child, etc.**

I.   Child Abuse

📖 If you suspect **abuse (physical, emotional, neglect, verbal, sexual, etc.) you are required to report it.***

📖 Be careful in **discussing discipline problems** with parents/ guardians that you suspect will **punish** the **child too severely**;

📖 Recognize that even though you must report suspected abuse, do **NOT assume** that **measures** will be taken to **help** the **child.**

📖 **Listen** to **children** even if you think they are exaggerating, to be sure that this is all that there is to their stories.

📖 **Document anecdotal records** of **repeated suspicions** such as bruises, unbathed conditions, etc. and **document** each time you **report** these **suspicions.**

📖 Do **NOT ignore** the **quiet, withdrawn students** in your classroom simply because these students present no discipline problems and bother no one in the classroom.

📖 If the parents/guardians find out (they should not **BUT**) that you reported your suspicions, be **prepared** that they may very well be **antagonistic.** Cover yourself by telling someone in administration or guidance.

📖 Do **NOT** talk to **children negatively** about their **parents**; even abused children will be **defensive** of their parents/guardians.

📖 Do not **practice corporal punishment, especially** with abused or special needs students.

📖 Always **error** on the side of **safety.**

*Reporting agencies for every state can be found at http://nccanch.acf.hhs.gov/general/legal/federal/index.cfm. Childhelp USA National Child Abuse Hotline is 1-800-4-ACHILD (1-800-422-4453), TDD: 1-800-2-A-CHILD.

II.   Student Suicide

- 📖 Learn the **warning signals** of **suicide** and never **ignore** them. See appendix.

- 📖 **Report in writing** your suspicions concerning a student's talk of suicide to the **principal** and/or **counselor** and/or **school nurse**.

- 📖 Do **NOT** take any **talk** or **threat** of suicide lightly regardless of the student's age.

- 📖 Watch for **dramatic changes** in **behavior** of students, such as, a gregarious student becoming withdrawn.

- 📖 Be willing to **listen** to troubled students.

- 📖 **Avoid** trying to make students think that their **problems** are **not serious**.

- 📖 If a student confides thoughts of suicide to you, **encourage** them **immediately** to talk to the **counselor** or **school psychologist**.

- 📖 Be **prepared** that the **student** or the **parents/guardians** may become **distressed** and/or **contentious** about you reporting your suspicion.

- 📖 If a **student** in your class should **commit suicide**, **insure** that the students in your class get **counseling** and **opportunities** to **talk** about their **feelings** and **reactions**.

- 📖 **Error** on the side of **safety**.

SUICIDE IS A PERMANENT SOLUTION
TO A TEMPORARY PROBLEM!

III. Violence

- **Know** and **follow** all of the **school guidelines** regarding violence, because they vary from school system to school system, state to state, etc.

- **Discuss conflict resolution** with students and do **role**-playing or other **activities** to **reinforce** how students can **deal with anger** other than violence.

- Try to **impede trouble** that may begin as a verbal argument, for example, **before** it can **escalate**.

- **Report** any "talk" or information that someone is carrying a **weapon** in **writing immediately** to the **principal** or **vice principal**.

- **Never** get **in between** two **combative** students, even young ladies.

- Send a **reliable student** for **help immediately**.

- Send students to the **office** one at a time (**separately**) that have been fighting or threatening to fight.

- Send a **referral** that **describes** what happened **in detail** by an uninvolved student **after** the students have been sent to the office.

- **Calm** your students and **return** to **classwork** without allowing discussion or sidetaking.

- Utilize opportunities to **support prevention** of violence in your school by **participating** in **programs** such as peer intervention, conflict resolution, etc.

IV. Invisible Student

- 📖 Make an effort to insure that **ALL** students **participate** in your classroom and do not ignore the students who are **quiet** and **withdrawn.**

- 📖 Call on **All** students by utilizing perhaps a **checklist** or **seating chart** and **checking names** as you call on students.

- 📖 Give students **time** to **think** about an **answer** by waiting a **reasonable** amount of **time** (use a **stopwatch** if you must to insure that you wait!)

- 📖 Use any window of **opportunity** such as recess or break time to **talk** to a shy, quiet, or **withdrawn student.**

- 📖 **Provide** classroom **opportunities** for students to utilize in **communication skills,** such as, oral reports, debates, plays, oral reading, historical news reporting, etc., in which **ALL** students participate.

- 📖 **Structure opportunities** to talk **individually** with **students,** such as, lunch in the cafeteria once a week with students, before school or after school homework help for ALL students, etc.

- 📖 Invite the quiet, shy student to the **parent/guardian conference** and **praise** them to their parents/guardians to **demonstrate** that you value the student.

- 📖 In **group activities,** give **All** students a **responsibility** that they need to discuss with their classmates.

- 📖 Make an **environment** in which students feel **safe** making a **mistake** or **having** their **own opinion** on a subject of discussion.

- 📖 **Encourage** students to be **accepting** of one another by being an **inclusive role model.**

V.   Teacher's Pet / Spoiled Child

📖 Encourage the student to **include others** when they are seeking personal attention, such as by asking another student or students to participate in the topic of conversation.

📖 **Plan activities that invite all students** to share their talents and good things that have happened to them, perhaps once a week on **Friday afternoons or once a month for older students.**

📖 **Allow all students to have opportunities** for one-on-one or small group discussions with the teacher such as mini-conferences about grades for example, lunch with the teacher in small groups once a week, etc.

📖 Plan activities that can be **shared with groups of parents**, grandparents, and significant others that display special talents such as plays, choral readings of poetry or prose, academic competitions, project exhibitions, holiday special programs, etc.

📖 Solicit the help of these students to **support students** who are perhaps more withdrawn by asking them to share a task to help the teacher, sending them together to accomplish an errand in another classroom, letting them peer tutor younger students, etc.

📖 Always **treat all students as though they are very special** to you to discourage any ideas that you favor any student over another.

📖 **Use classroom management fairly and consistently** to discourage student perceptions of partiality.

📖 **At the end of the week send home coupons, notes, small certificates for all of your students to "brag"** about things they have done that you are proud that they have accomplished, etc.

- Allow **each child** the opportunity to be **a helper**. Withdraw the privilege only if the student does not act responsibly.

- **Solicit the help of counselors, principal, vice principals**, etc. to take time from their busy schedules to meet with each of your students once a month for one-to-one conversations.

- Always be eager to **shower your attention on all students** because for some students you may be the only adult who does so.

The two worst things a parent can give a young person are

MONEY and WHEELS!

The two most important things a parent can give a child are

ROOTS and WINGS!

~~After Hodding Carter

VI. Disabled/Diverse Learners

- Seek the **guidance of the professionals** in your school for suggestions on how best to meet the needs of a particular student who is a diverse learner.

- Present lessons in a **variety of ways** to appeal to the auditory, visual, kinesthetic, interpersonal, mathematical, musical, etc. learners and to help make learning more interesting for all of your students.

- **Create individual instruction** plans for all of your students by using software programs designed for this purpose or create your own templates for accomplishing this task in less time.

- Provide opportunities for students to work **at their own pace.**

- **Model learning strategies** with students such as S4R by surveying, reading, writing, recalling, and reviewing with the students.

- Encourage **peer tutoring** and utilize **cooperative learning** to create a supportive framework for all students.

- Create **open-ended activities** for students that allow them to select the way in which they will complete an assignment.

- Provide open-ended group projects that allow students to brainstorm and display the talents of individuals in the group in ways that **an individual student may choose to share.**

- **Go to inservices, workshops,** or take classes to familiarize yourself with current strategies for meeting the needs of diverse learners.

- **Respect all students' capabilities** and provide them with the best opportunities for learning to the best of your ability.

VII. ADHD (Attention Deficit Hyperactive Disorder)

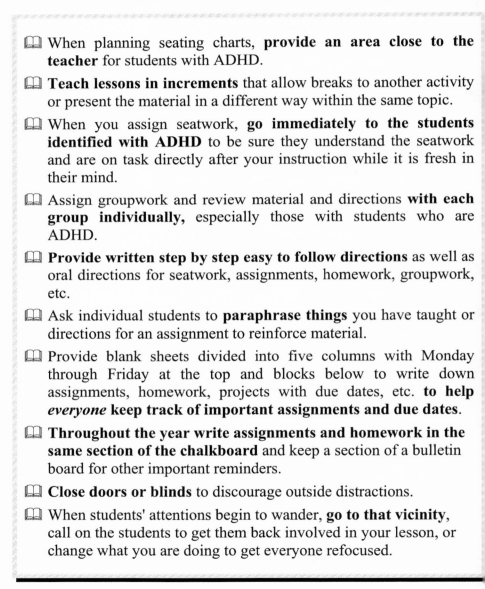

- When planning seating charts, **provide an area close to the teacher** for students with ADHD.
- **Teach lessons in increments** that allow breaks to another activity or present the material in a different way within the same topic.
- When you assign seatwork, **go immediately to the students identified with ADHD** to be sure they understand the seatwork and are on task directly after your instruction while it is fresh in their mind.
- Assign groupwork and review material and directions **with each group individually,** especially those with students who are ADHD.
- **Provide written step by step easy to follow directions** as well as oral directions for seatwork, assignments, homework, groupwork, etc.
- Ask individual students to **paraphrase things** you have taught or directions for an assignment to reinforce material.
- Provide blank sheets divided into five columns with Monday through Friday at the top and blocks below to write down assignments, homework, projects with due dates, etc. **to help** *everyone* **keep track of important assignments and due dates.**
- **Throughout the year write assignments and homework in the same section of the chalkboard** and keep a section of a bulletin board for other important reminders.
- **Close doors or blinds** to discourage outside distractions.
- When students' attentions begin to wander, **go to that vicinity,** call on the students to get them back involved in your lesson, or change what you are doing to get everyone refocused.

VIII. Mild or Moderate Mentally Retarded

📖 **Consult with the professionals for strategies** to help these students.

📖 Provide a **variety of ways** for students to complete projects that will encourage individuality and personal strengths.

📖 **Utilize computer technology** and excellent educational software that allows students to work at their own pace and/or at their level of **performance.**

📖 **Make a general check of homework** or assignment sheets as students are writing them down to determine that all students have written them down correctly.

📖 If a teacher's aide is not provided, **solicit the help of parents**, the special education resource teacher, education students at the local college, or retirees in the community to assist with individualizing education for **all** the students.

📖 **Utilize peer tutoring** and cooperative groups to help these students be successful in the classroom.

📖 **Teach songs, mnemonic devices, poems, acronyms**, and other such devices to help all students with memorization or to learn procedures, etc.

📖 **Utilize repetition, hands-on, experiential learning to reinforce concepts.**

📖 **Be fair and above all be consistent** with classroom management and procedures/routines of the classroom.

📖 **Model acceptance and encourage a supportive and reassuring environment participated in by all students.**

IX.   Gifted Students

- Provide a **creative environment** that encourages independence.

- Encourage gifted students to be **supportive of others** through peer **tutoring.**

- **Create open-ended assignments** and projects that allow students to select creative and experiential alternatives.

- Seek opportunities to allow **independent work** that facilitates exploration and creativity.

- **Pursue sharing of ideas though discussion**, individual oral presentations, debates, panels, small group discussion, etc.

- **Utilize technology** such as the Internet and excellent educational software programs that allow for creativity and exploration of various topics.

- Encourage students to complete **class projects** such as a monthly classroom newspaper, writing and performing a play, historical enactments, etc.

- Arrange for a means by which students may **publish their creative writing** either in actual publication forums or a **classroom created publication or personally developed books.**

- **Display artwork, photography, and original writings** to support all of the students' endeavors.

- **Provide opportunities that students' work can be viewed by other classes**, administrators, parents and other family members, etc.

X. Public Education Means Teaching All the Students

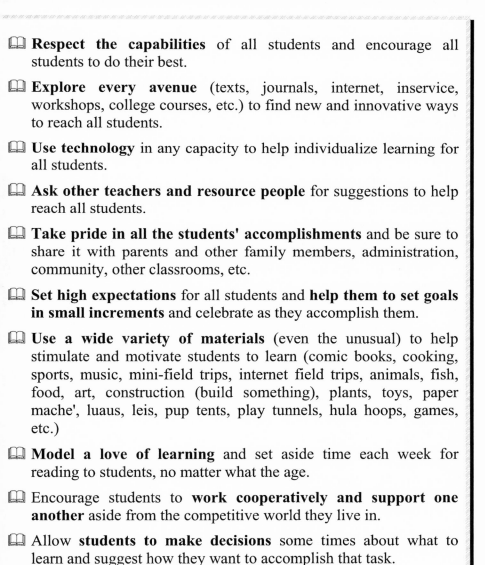

📖 **Respect the capabilities** of all students and encourage all students to do their best.

📖 **Explore every avenue** (texts, journals, internet, inservice, workshops, college courses, etc.) to find new and innovative ways to reach all students.

📖 **Use technology** in any capacity to help individualize learning for all students.

📖 **Ask other teachers and resource people** for suggestions to help reach all students.

📖 **Take pride in all the students' accomplishments** and be sure to share it with parents and other family members, administration, community, other classrooms, etc.

📖 **Set high expectations** for all students and **help them to set goals in small increments** and celebrate as they accomplish them.

📖 **Use a wide variety of materials** (even the unusual) to help stimulate and motivate students to learn (comic books, cooking, sports, music, mini-field trips, internet field trips, animals, fish, food, art, construction (build something), plants, toys, paper mache', luaus, leis, pup tents, play tunnels, hula hoops, games, etc.)

📖 **Model a love of learning** and set aside time each week for reading to students, no matter what the age.

📖 Encourage students to **work cooperatively and support one another** aside from the competitive world they live in.

📖 Allow **students to make decisions** some times about what to learn and suggest how they want to accomplish that task.

<u>Notes</u>

Notes

References and Resources

Books:

📖 Allain, Violet Anselmini, *Teaching Diverse Student: Preparing with Cases*. Bloomington, IN: Phi Delta Kappa Educational Foundation, 1998.

📖 Blackburn, Jack E., *One At A Time: The Creative Teacher's Guide to Individualized Instruction Without Anarchy*. Pacific Palisades, CA, Goodyear Publishing Company, 1976.

📖 Bowers, C. A., *Culturally Responsive Teaching and Supervision: A Handbook for Staff Development*. New York: Teachers College Press, 1991.

📖 Cramer, Sharon F., *Collaboration: A Success Strategy for Special Educators*. Boston: Allyn and Bacon, 1998.

📖 Glennon, Will, *200 Ways to Raise A Girl's Self-Esteem*. Berkeley, CA: Conari Press distributed by Publishers Group West, 1999.

📖 Kenner, Charmian, *Home Pages: Literacy Links for Bilingual Children*. Stokes-on-Kent, England: Trentham Books, 2000.

📖 McEwan, Elaine K., *When Kids Say No to School: Helping Children At-Risk of Failure, Refusal, or Dropping Out*. Wheaton, IL: H. Shaw Publishers, 1998.

📖 McNamara, Barry E., *Keys to Parenting a Child With a Learning Disability*. Hauppauge, NY: Barron's Publishing, 1995.

📖 Olson, Judy L., *Teaching Children and Adolescents With Special Needs*. Upper Saddle River, NJ: Merrill Publishing, 2000.

📖 Pianta, Robert C., *Enhancing Relationships Between Children and Teachers*. Washington D.C.: American Psychological Association, 1999.

📖 Pianta, Robert C., *High-Risk Children in School: Constructing Sustaining Relationships*. Washington D.C.: American Psychological Assn., 1996.

📖 Smith, Sally Liberman, *No Easy Answers: The Learning Disabled Child at Home and at School*. New York: Bantam Books, 1995.

📖 Tuttle, Cheryl Gerson, *Parenting a Child With a Learning Disability: A Practical, Empathetic Guide*. New York: Doubleday Publishing, 1995.

Journals and Magazines:

📖 **Exceptional Children:** Council for Exceptional Children; 1920 Association Drive, Reston, VA 22091; http://www.cec.sped.org/ec-jour.htm E-mail: cecpubs@cec.sped.org; Phone: 703-620-3660, quarterly.

📖 **Journal For The Education of the Gifted**: Prufrock Press; Association for the Gifted; PO Box 8813, Waco, TX 76714-8813; http://www.prufrock.com; 800-998-2208

📖 **Journal of Education for Students Placed at Risk**: Lawrence Erlbaum Associates, Inc., 10 Industrial Ave, Mahwah, NJ 07430-2262; http://www.erlbaum.com/Journals/journals/JESPAR/jespar.htm; journals@erlbaum.com; 800-926-6579, quarterly.

📖 **Journal of Educational and Psychological Consultation**: Lawrence Erlbaum Associates, Inc. Association for Educational and Psychological Consultants, 10 Industrial Ave, Mahwah, NJ 07430-2262; http://www.erlbaum.com; journals@erlbaum.com; 201-236-9500 , quarterly.

📖 **Journal of Educational Psychology**: American Psychological Association, 750 First St, N E, Washington, DC 20002-4242; http://www.apa.org/journals/edu.html; subscriptions@apa.org; 202-336-5600 quarterly.

📖 **Journal of Learning Disabilities**: Pro-Ed Inc. 8700 Shoal Creek Blvd, Austin, TX 78757-6897; http://www.proedinc.com; proed1@aol.com; 512-451-3246, bi-monthly.

📖 **Journal of Learning Disabilities**: Sage Publications Ltd.; 6 Bonhill St, London, EC2A 4PU, United Kingdom; http://www.sagepub.co.uk/; market@sagepub.co.uk, Phone: 44-20-7330-1266, quarterly.

📖 **Remedial and Special Education**: Pro-Ed Inc., 8700 Shoal Creek Blvd, Austin, TX 78757-6897; http://www.proedinc.com/; proed1@aol.com; 512-451-3246, bi-monthly.

📖 More online at **http://www.publist.com**

Internet Sites:

📖 **Achievement Gaps, NEA,** http://www.achievementgaps.org/

📖 **CLWG: Children's Literature Web Guide**, Internet resources for children's books, http://www.acs.ucalgary.ca/~dkbrown/index/html

📖 **Dave's ESL Café**, http://www.daveseslcafe.com/

📖 **EduHound.com Espanol**, www.eduhound.com/espanol/defaultEN.cfm

📖 **ESL PartyLand**, http://www.eslpartyland.com/

📖 **EslGames.com**, http://eslgames.com

📖 **Family Education**, helping teachers, children and their parents/guardians, http://www.familyeducation.com

📖 **Guidance Online**, http://home.cfl.rr.com/nwunder/guidance.html

📖 **Guide to Legal Rights of Public School Students with Disabilities**, http://www.dralegal.org/publications/Public_Schools_Guide

📖 **National Association for Gifted Children**, http://www.nagc.org/

📖 **NEA: Issues**, http://www.nea.org/issues

📖 **Office of Special Education Programs (OSEP)**, http://www.ed.gov/offices/OSERS/OSEP/index.html

📖 **Reform Nationwide**, making schools work better for all children, http://www.edreform.com/pubs/stxsts97.htm

📖 **SERI - Special Education Resources on the Internet**, http://www.hood/edu/seri/serihome.htm

📖 **U.S. Department of Education**, links to programs, policy, etc., http://www.ed.gov

Chapter 12: Professionalism

Is teaching a profession? This question has been discussed and researched very heavily over the past four decades. Dozens of criteria exist which help to define a full profession. However, the four that are most commonly cited are:

1.) <u>Autonomy</u> - members of a profession control entry into a field and regulate practice by means of an ethical code.

2.) <u>Expert Knowledge</u>, practice is based on an established body of knowledge, which is not shared by those outside of the profession.

3.) <u>Extensive Education</u> - expertise is initially acquired through a prolonged period of professional study.

4.) <u>Service Orientation</u> - the profession sees itself, and is seen by others, as performing a vital service to clients and to society.

Using these criteria, teaching has been appropriately described as an **emerging profession**. It appears to be on the cusp of entering alongside professions such as medicine, law and engineering. This chapter will outline numerous suggestions on how to be a viable professional working in the field of teaching. Placed directly in the center of the movement to elevate teaching to a full profession is the concept of **Lifelong Learning**. Teachers must dedicate themselves to learning and growth if they are going to be thought of in the same breath as physicians, attorneys and engineers.

I. Join and Support Professional Groups

- Join the **Parent-Teacher Organization** at your school and actively participate so that you can interact more with the best education PR persons, parents.

- **Join or start a group in your school system** or individual school that promotes the profession with workshops, guest speakers, in-services, etc.

- Find a professional group that meets monthly or quarterly that engages in **professional activities** that expand your profession and join.

- Join the local unit of the **National Education Association** or the **American Federation of Teachers** to receive their publications concerning innovations, political issues, etc. that effect your profession.

- Join a professional organization that specializes in the area in which you teach (**e.g. International Reading Association**, etc.)

- Join a professional group that sets standards in your profession such as the **Interstate New Teacher Assessment** and Support Consortium.

- Join a community organization that supports professionals in your community to help promote the education profession by **serving as its representative**.

- Find out who is in charge of **programs for an organization** and offer suggestions for topics, issues, concerns, speakers, etc. that you would like to hear about at meetings (usually a very welcome offer to these persons).

📖 **Promote membership amongst your peers** in organizations that you believe truly foster the education profession.

📖 Whatever organizations you select, be sure to **attend meetings** on a regular basis and consider actively working within the organizations that you choose to join.

WE CAN MAKE A DIFFERENCE!

I have come to the frightening conclusion that I am the decisive element in the classroom.

It's my personal approach

that creates the climate.

It's my daily mood that makes the weather.

As a teacher, I possess a tremendous power to make a tool of torture

or an instrument of inspiration.

I can humiliate or humor, hurt or heal.

In all situations, it is my response that decides whether a crisis will be escalated or deescalated and a child humanized or de-humanized.

~~Haim Ginot

II. Mentor

- 📖 **Offer sincere and concrete support to all new faculty** at your school.

- 📖 **Contribute to and update any faculty handbooks** and if there is none, initiate one.

- 📖 **Volunteer to be a mentor** to a specific new faculty member.

- 📖 **Offer constructive criticism** when asked to review lesson plans, field trip plans, etc.

- 📖 **Be a good listener for the new faculty** member to bounce ideas off or just vent frustration.

- 📖 **Offer to share materials** and planning with the new faculty member.

- 📖 **Be a positive role model** for the new faculty member by presenting the best of the profession.

- 📖 **Encourage the new faculty member to try new ideas** they may have and be open to new innovations that they may want to share with you and your students.

- 📖 **Encourage other veteran colleagues to become mentors** to new faculty.

- 📖 **Provide mentorship to those colleagues** who decide to become mentors to new faculty.

III. Write About Teaching

📖 Remember to follow **school district policy** in regards to **media contact.**

📖 **Send positive letters** about your classroom to the local newspaper, etc.

📖 **Write positive articles** about teaching and send them **to journals or teaching magazines.**

📖 **Respond to "Letters to the Editor"** that negatively respond to the teaching profession.

📖 **Write to politicians** and voice your opinion during crucial campaigns that will make a difference to teaching.

📖 **Write letters home to the parents of your students** to let them know the positive things that are going on in teaching and to solicit their help during elections, etc.

📖 **Write material to be used in your classroom** to help your students learn from their teacher, as opposed to a textbook.

📖 **Write articles concerning your area of teaching** and submit them to journals specifically designed for your teaching area.

📖 **Combine writing efforts with other teachers** to address a specific issue or area of teaching and select the best avenue to publish it.

📖 **Submit articles to one journal at a time,** but don't be discouraged by rejections. Send it to the next choice on your list.

📖 **Submit written material often** (you are modeling something important for your students) and the more you submit, the better your chances of publication.

IV. Attend and Be Active in Community

- 📖 **Be alert to activities in the community** that give your classroom and your school opportunities to be represented in a positive arena, such as fairs, competitions, etc.

- 📖 **Attend activities in neighboring communities** in which schools are featured to get ideas for things that could be done by your school or school system.

- 📖 Try to attend community activities to make you **a visible and viable member of the community**.

- 📖 **Volunteer to help with some community activities** in whatever way you may be able. It sets a good example when your school or school system requests volunteers.

- 📖 Promote activities in your school or school system that the community can participate in such as **blood drives, book fairs,** etc.

- 📖 Although time may not permit always attending, make an effort to attend **town meetings** to help yourself be more aware of concerns and activities going on in your community.

- 📖 **Rally the support of the Parent Teacher Organization** for community projects that will be beneficial to your school system and the community at large.

- 📖 **Consider working for voter registration** or supporting the community in worthwhile campaigns and educating the public on the issues during election periods.

- 📖 **Send pictures with captions frequently to the local newspaper of the students in your classroom** or activities in your school to help keep the community aware of your school and the positive things that are happening there.

📖 **Frequently give letter writing assignments** to your students to thank members of the community for things that they have done to help the community be a better place for children to grow up.

THE IMPORTANCE OF PARENTS!

Parents are their children's first and most influential teachers.

What parents do to help their children is more important to the academic success ...

than how well off the family is!

V. Continue Your Education

- 📖 **Participate in workshops, in-services,** etc. in your area of teaching.

- 📖 **Take classes at the local college or university** in an area that will enhance your teaching.

- 📖 **Pursue the highest degree that you can in your area** because your students deserve to have the best prepared teacher. Most school systems offer some type of reciprocity of tuition.

- 📖 **Read books, journals, etc.** that concern education in general, your specific area of teaching, and such related topics to stay current in your field.

- 📖 Consider **developing your own presentation** concerning an issue in education, your specific area of teaching, etc. to share with others.

- 📖 Consider **teaching as an adjunct professor at the local college or university** to give you insight and perhaps a new perspective **of the teaching profession.**

- 📖 **Take a course totally for your personal enjoyment** and to help to make you a more rounded individual.

- 📖 **Take a course that supports your teaching** such as a technology course.

- 📖 **Be open-minded concerning new innovations** in teaching and learn to use them before making judgments that they are not helpful to your teaching.

- 📖 **Look for opportunities to introduce and develop new courses** into the curriculum at your school.

VI. Read Professional Journals

📖 **Subscribe to professional journals in your area of teaching.** You many need to **join** the **professional organization** to subscribe to some of the professional journals.

📖 **Subscribe to professional journals that have general articles** concerning the teaching profession.

📖 If you can't afford to subscribe to so many journals, **ask the local librarian or the school librarian to subscribe to journals** that they may not carry that are of particular interest to you.

📖 **Read professional journals at the local library or in the professional library** of your school or school system.

📖 As you read professional journals, **look for topics that you may be interested in writing about** that are not discussed in the way that you would plan to write about it.

📖 **Look for material that suggests ways that you might improve your teaching.** For example, much research has revealed patterns in ways that teachers call on students and teachers can use that research to help them be more aware of avoiding such patterns.

📖 **Look for ideas for other reading materials** (books, pamphlets, teaching materials, etc.).

📖 As you read professional journals, **look for new trends in education** that may suggest courses or other ways to make you current in your profession.

📖 Be an advocate and example of professional reading by **sharing well written and pertinent articles with peers.** Perhaps make copies of a really germane article and put one in your colleagues' mailboxes.

🕮 Be an advocate and encourage others not just to read the journals but also to **write and submit materials to the journals.**

DESIRE

IS THE INGREDIENT

THAT CHANGES THE WARM

WATER OF MEDIOCRITY

TO THE STEAM OF

OUTSTANDING SUCCESS!

- Anonymous

VII.   Develop an Expertise and Share It

- Become an expert in a particular area concerning teaching, an issue in teaching, or your area of teaching.

- Inject humor into your topic. Teachers love humor!

- Make offers to share that information with others at your school, your school system, or other schools and school systems.

- Look for arenas to present your material to others, such as education conventions, etc.

- Volunteer to teach a particular unit germane to more than one area of teaching that you have developed particularly well to other teachers' classes.

- Learn to use technology presentation software programs to help you to enhance your presentations.

- Utilize time off during breaks, summer, etc. to expand and improve upon your presentation.

- Enlist the help of the inservice department of the local college or university to seek out audiences for your particular expert presentation.

- Encourage and assist colleagues to do similar projects in an area of interest to them.

- Team up with colleagues to do such presentation projects together.

VIII. Seek National Certification

- 📖 Learn what is required to attain **National Certification**. Visit the website of the **National Board of Professional Teaching Standards** at http://www.nbpts.org/.

- 📖 **Try to produce several videotapes** of a particular lesson to get one most desirable copy.

- 📖 **Take volumes of pictures** of your students at work and your bulletin boards, etc.

- 📖 Over time teachers should **collect** examples of students' work.

- 📖 **Keep copies of publications** that you have had, even small newspaper pictures with captions.

- 📖 Teachers should keep files of **successful lesson plans**, lesson units, etc.

- 📖 Teachers should keep **files of correspondence** to and from parents and guardians.

- 📖 **Invite the principal, vice principal, other teachers, parents, etc.** into your classroom often to overcome the "visitor jitters."

- 📖 **Be sure to keep records of any recognition's and honors** you have had.

- 📖 **Keep records of activities** that you have had your classes participate in, community work you have done, volunteer efforts, in-services, workshops, etc.

IX. Be a Politically Savvy Professional

📖 Read materials that present the **views of political candidates** concerning education.

📖 **Watch television and listen to radio programs that feature politicians and their views during campaigns.**

📖 **Pay attention to the groups that represent teachers** and the information that they often summarize to help teachers discern the candidates and their positions regarding teaching.

📖 **Share information** with colleagues.

📖 **Speak to parents at the Parent Teacher Organization meetings** concerning the issues related to the schools and enlist their support of the candidates that best support education issues.

📖 **Volunteer to help with voter registration,** etc.

📖 **Actively write and encourage others to write to politicians** concerning issues of importance to you and your school system.

📖 **Consider helping with the campaign of a politician** that supports education issues.

📖 **Financially support the campaigns of politicians** that have **education** as a **high priority.**

📖 **Do not lodge yourself into one political camp.** Try to gain an understanding of which politicians truly support teachers and education.

X.   Promote Your Profession

📖 **Always speak highly of your profession** in social gatherings and about the community.

📖 **Encourage your colleagues to be positive** when they speak of the teaching profession in the community, in writing, etc.

📖 **Encourage young adults to pursue a career in teaching** in view of the fact that things have changed dramatically (they still have room for improvement) in teaching that are very positive.

📖 **Contribute to or initiate a school newspaper or school system newsletter** that informs parents and the community about the positive things that are happening in your school or school system.

📖 **Listen carefully to the opinions of others** and be ready to admit when there are problems and then commit yourself to making things better in your profession.

📖 **Be sure to defend your school and school system or the American education system** if it is wrongfully attacked (be prepared by doing the reading and writing that make you a knowledgeable defender).

📖 Spread the good news in the community about the **accomplishments and positive activities of colleagues** in your profession.

📖 **Encourage parents and guardians to spend time in your classroom** to observe the positive happenings of your school or school system.

📖 **Consider inviting members of the community to participate in your classroom as speakers,** observers, teachers of special topics, etc., to help share the positive nature of your school and school system.

📖 **Always speak highly of the community in which you teach** and perhaps also live. It is without a doubt unfair to expect the support of the community if you and your colleagues do not give that support to the community.

RISK

To hope is to risk despair, and to try is to risk failure.

But risks must be taken,

because the greatest risk in life is to risk nothing!

The person who risks nothing, does nothing, has nothing,

is nothing, and becomes nothing!

He may avoid suffering and sorrow,

but he simply cannot learn and feel,

and change and grow, and love and live!

Chained by his certitudes, he's a slave.

He's forfeited his freedom.

Only the person who risks is truly free!

Try it and see what happens!

~~Leo Buscaglia

<u>Notes</u>

<u>Notes</u>

References and Resources

Books:

📖 Banner, James M., *The Elements of Teaching*. New Haven, CT: Yale University Press, 1999.

📖 Dimock, Elna M., *Teacher Certification Tests*. New York: Arco Publishing, 1999.

📖 Duke, Daniel Linden, *Teaching - The Imperiled Profession*. Albany, NY: State University of New York Press, 1984.

📖 Erickson, Lawrence G., *Supervision of Literacy Programs: Teachers as Grass-Roots Change Agents*. Boston: Allyn and Bacon, 1995.

📖 Etheridge, Carol Plata, et al., *Challenge to Change: The Memphis Experience with School-Based Decision Making*. Washington, D.C.: National Education Association, 1993.

📖 Finkel, Donald L., *Educating for Freedom: The Paradox of Pedagogy*. New Brunswick, NJ: Rutgers University Press, 1995.

📖 Fullan, Michael, *What's Worth Fighting For in Your School?* New York: Teachers College Press, 1996.

📖 Major, Cherie and Robert Pines, editors, *Teaching to Teach: New Partnerships in Teacher Education*. Washington, D.C.: National Education Association, 1999.

📖 Murray, Frank, editor, *The Teacher Educator's Handbook: Building a Knowledge Base for the Preparation of Teachers*. San Francisco: Jossey-Bass, 1996.

📖 Shedd, Joseph B., *Tangled Hierarchies: Teachers as Professionals and the Management of Schools*. San Francisco: Jossey-Bass Publishers, 1991.

Sparks, Langer, Georgea, et al, *Teaching as Decision Making: Successful Practices for the Secondary Teacher*. Upper Saddle River, NJ: Prentice Hall, 2000

Sullo, Robert A., *The Inspiring Teacher: New Beginnings for the 21st Century*. New York: NEA Professional Library, 1999.

WeinlanderAlbertina Abrams, *How To Prepare for the National Teacher Examinations, NTE: Core Battery and Specialty Area Tests*. Hauppage, NY: Barron's Educational Series, 1992.

Journals and Magazines:

Classroom Leadership: Association for Supervision and Curriculum Development;: 1703 N Beauregard St, Alexandria, VA 22314; **E-mail**: update@ascd.org; **Phone**: 703-578-9600

Critical Issues in Teacher Education: Illinois Association of Teacher Education; Dept of Student Teaching, Eastern Illinois University, Charleston, IL 61920; **E-mail**: cfmev@eju.edu; **Phone**: 618-242-3454

ED Initiatives: U.S. Department of Education, Federal Office Bldg 6, Rm 7W114, 400 Maryland Ave, S W, Washington, DC 20202; E-mail: kirk_winters@ed.gov; Phone: 202-401-3132

Educational Leadership and Administration: Caddo Gap Press; California Association of Professors of Educational Administration, 3145 Geary Blvd, Ste 275, San Francisco, CA 94118; E-mail: caddogap@aol.com; Phone: 415-922-1911.

Educational Leadership: ASCD, PO Box 79760, Baltimore, MD, 21279-0760; http://www.ascd.org; E-mail: member@ascd.org; Phone: 703-578-9600.

More online at **http://www.publist.com**

Internet Sites:

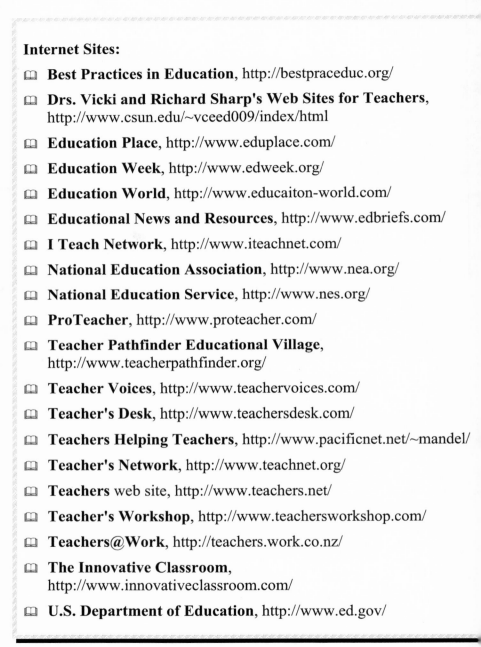

- **Best Practices in Education**, http://bestpraceduc.org/
- **Drs. Vicki and Richard Sharp's Web Sites for Teachers**, http://www.csun.edu/~vceed009/index/html
- **Education Place**, http://www.eduplace.com/
- **Education Week**, http://www.edweek.org/
- **Education World**, http://www.educaiton-world.com/
- **Educational News and Resources**, http://www.edbriefs.com/
- **I Teach Network**, http://www.iteachnet.com/
- **National Education Association**, http://www.nea.org/
- **National Education Service**, http://www.nes.org/
- **ProTeacher**, http://www.proteacher.com/
- **Teacher Pathfinder Educational Village**, http://www.teacherpathfinder.org/
- **Teacher Voices**, http://www.teachervoices.com/
- **Teacher's Desk**, http://www.teachersdesk.com/
- **Teachers Helping Teachers**, http://www.pacificnet.net/~mandel/
- **Teacher's Network**, http://www.teachnet.org/
- **Teachers** web site, http://www.teachers.net/
- **Teacher's Workshop**, http://www.teachersworkshop.com/
- **Teachers@Work**, http://teachers.work.co.nz/
- **The Innovative Classroom**, http://www.innovativeclassroom.com/
- **U.S. Department of Education**, http://www.ed.gov/

Appendix I

Difficult Interview Questions

1. What is your philosophy of education?
2. What if ....?
3. How would you set up a program in your major teaching area?
4. What are your weaknesses?
5. Define the role of the principal.
6. Describe yourself using five adjectives.
7. How do you handle discipline in your classroom?
8. Do you want students to like you?
9. Describe in detail a lesson that you taught.
10. What are your strengths?

Anthony, Rebecca and Steve Head, National Teacher Interview Survey.

ASCUS Research Report, 1990, page 5.

Appendix II

Sample Questions to Ask at the Interview*

1. Do I have grade level curriculum guides?

2. May I get a copy of the school's rules and procedures?

3. Are there opportunities to work with extracurricular activities?

4. Is there any extra classroom help?

5. What technology equipment is in the classroom? What technology equipment is available for loan to the classroom?

6. What classroom supplies will be available through the school?

7. How much money will I receive for supplies?

8. What duties will I have (bus, cafeteria, etc.)?

9. What are the ethnic backgrounds of the students?

10. Will I be encouraged to utilize cooperative learning, team teaching, local outdoor excursions, cross-age peer tutoring, etc. (anything you want to use in your classroom that you do not want questioned or prohibited after you start teaching!).

*Anna Marie DiCesare, Florida Southern College, Seminar for Interns during Student Teaching

Appendix III

Characteristics Which School Systems Value

1. **The Ability to Make a Difference in a Student's Life.** All those who are involved with school systems want teacher in their classrooms who sincerely like children and who are willing to work to see those children succeed.

2. **A Variety of Life Experience.** School Systems look for teachers who bring with them a variety of experiences. Recent graduates whose resumes include volunteer work, camp counseling and community work strike a responsive chord in the hiring office.

3. **Managing a Classroom.** If you haven't taken a course in classroom management, you probably should, because school administrators are looking for evidence that you understand the task.

4. **Student Teaching Experience.** Administrators place strong emphasis on the evaluations you receive from your student teaching experience, so make the most of it.

5. **Academic Preparation.** New certification requirements in nearly every state place increased emphasis on strong academic preparation.

6. **Personal Appearance.** Like it or not, first impressions are important. Teacher candidates must present a professional appearance for interviews.

7. **A Sense of Humor.** New teachers need to be able to laugh - at both situations and themselves - recognizing that they are human and can make mistakes, just as students do.

8. **Adaptability.** Administrators seek teachers who are able to bend, but not break. They look for assurance that you have demonstrated that you can withstand the pressures of the job.

9. **Maturity.** Accountability and evaluation are increasingly important to school systems. Administrators want teachers who are able to withstand scrutiny and take criticism.

10. **Involvement.** Teachers are expected to be active and assume leadership roles in the community. Administrators look for teachers who are willing to come in early and stay late.

Gene Parker, Director, Career Planning and Placement, West Texas State University. The Job Search Handbook for Educators 1992 ASCUS Annual: Association for School, College and University Staffing, Inc. 1992, page 4.

Appendix IV

Bloom's Revised Taxonomy

Highest level	Create	New ideas, products, or ways of looking at things
High	Evaluate	Check, hypothesize, critique, experiment, judge.
Low-high	Analyze	Compare, explore, organize, question, deconstruct
Above-low	Apply	Implement, utilize, execute.
Low	Understand	Explain, interpret, summarize, paraphrase, classify.
Lowest	Remember	Recognize, list, name, describe, tell, recall.

Unclear Objectives	Revised Objectives
Students will know the dates of important events in U.S. History.	Each student will *recall* the 10 major events of the Civil War.
Students will know described cases of mental disorders.	Each student will *classify* observed or described cases of mental disorders.
Students will understand the relevant and irrelevant numbers in a mathematical word problem.	Each student will *distinguish* between relevant and irrelevant numbers in a mathematical word problem.
Students will know the best way to solve the word problem.	Each student will *judge* which of the two methods is the best way to solve the word problem.

http://coe.sdsu.edu/eet/Articles/bloomrev/index.htm

The Revised Bloom's Taxonomy Table						
The Knowledge Dimension	The Cognitive Process Dimension					
	Remember	Understand	Apply	Analyze	Evaluate	Create
Factual Knowledge						
Conceptual Knowledge						
Procedural Knowledge						
Meta-Cognitive Knowledge						
Source: http://coe.sdsu.edu/eet/Articles/bloomrev/index.htm						

Appendix V

The Suicide Prevention Resource Center guidelines for teachers provide the following warning signals of suicide and should not be ignored:

Teachers should be aware of the following behaviors that may indicate suicidal tendencies:

- A suddenly deteriorating academic performance.

- Self-mutilation.

- A fixation with death or violence.

- Unhealthy peer relationships.

- Volatile mood swings or a sudden change in personality.

- Indications that the student is in an unhealthy, destructive, or abusive relationship.

- Risk-taking behaviors.

- Signs of an eating disorder.

- Difficulty in adjusting to gender identity.

- Bullying.

- Depression. Symptoms of depression include the following:

    o A sudden worsening in academic performance

    o Withdrawal from friends and extracurricular activities

    o Expressions of sadness and hopelessness, or anger and rage

    o A sudden decline in enthusiasm and energy

    o Overreaction to criticism

    o Lowered self-esteem, or feelings of guilt

    o Indecision, lack of concentration, and forgetfulness

    o Restlessness and agitation

Chalking It Up To Experience

- o   Changes in eating or sleeping patterns

- o   Unprovoked episodes of crying

- o   Sudden neglect of appearance and hygiene

- o   Fatigue

- o   The abuse of alcohol or other drugs as young people try to "self-medicate" their emotional pain

Some warning signs of suicide demand immediate action:

- Talking or writing about suicide or death

- Giving direct verbal cues, such as "I wish I were dead" and "I'm going to end it all"

- Giving less direct verbal cues, such as "You will be better off without me," "What's the point of living?", "Soon you won't have to worry about me," and "Who cares if I'm dead, anyway?"

- Isolating him- or herself from friends and family

- Expressing the belief that life is meaningless

- Giving away prized possessions

- Exhibiting a sudden and unexplained improvement in mood after being depressed or withdrawn

- Neglecting his or her appearance and hygiene

- Dropping out of school or social, athletic, and/or community activities

- Obtaining a weapon (such as a firearm) or another means of hurting him- or herself (such as prescription medications)

Available at http://www.sprc.org/featured_resources/customized/teachers.asp#warningsigns.

Appendix VI

Discipline Reporting Form

The action took place:

1. **Classroom** _____
2. **Hallway** _____
3. **Outside** _____
4. **Cafeteria** _____
5. **Other** _____

The action involved:

- **Another student** _____ **Specific** _____
- **No other students**

Specific Behavior:

1. **Use of inappropriate language** _____ **Specifics** _____

2. **Inappropriate behavior** _____

   - **Talking during instruction** _____
   - **Out of seat during instruction** _____
   - **Taking other students belongings** ____ **Specifics** _____
   - **Hitting a classmate** _____ **Specifics** _____
   - **Fighting with a classmate** ____ **Specifics** _____
   - **Damaging school property:**
     - **Desk** ____ **Specifics** _____
     - **Wall** ____ **Specifics** _____
     - **Outside building** _____ **Specifics**

Biographical Information

Perry A. Castelli is an experienced classroom teacher with twenty plus years of practice across the K-12 grade levels. He earned a B.S. in Music Education and Speech Minor from Kent State University in Kent, Ohio. He began his teaching career in Cleveland, Ohio serving several years as an elementary and middle school music teacher. During this time he earned a M.S. in Theoretical Foundations of Education from Kent State University.

Moving to the greater Baltimore, Maryland area, his next teaching assignment was at the high and middle school levels teaching music and English courses, coaching two sports and assisting in the production of musicals. During this time he earned a Ph.D. from the University of Maryland, College Park in Social Foundations of Education.

After earning his Ph.D., he spent ten years as coordinator of secondary education for the Troy State University School of Education in Troy, Alabama. He taught undergraduate and graduate courses in the foundations of education and educational leadership. He also taught for Troy State University in Oahu, Hawaii; Guantanamo Bay, Cuba; Key West and Orlando, Florida; Atlanta, Georgia; and Montgomery, Alabama.

Fall 1998, he was appointed dean of the School of Education at Barton College in Wilson, North Carolina, where he enjoyed working with an outstanding faculty. Together they worked toward the institution of a new chapter of Kappa Delta Pi, the implementation of new programs in SLD and Early Childhood education, construction of a new Education building, and other numerous accomplishments.

In the summer of 2001, he was appointed chair of the Department of Education at Florida Southern College, Lakeland, Florida. He has been the recipient of "outstanding teaching" awards at every level of education. His current research and presentation topics include: Classroom Management, Stress and Time Management for Teachers, Stress Management and Time Management for First Year Medical Students, School Law, Preventing Teen Suicides, Improving Home/School Relations, and Preparing Teachers Today for Tomorrow's Schools. He has presented these workshops throughout the Southeast region of the United States.

Vivian L. Castelli is an experienced classroom teacher with sixteen years practice across the K-12 grade levels. After earning a B.S. in Elementary Education from Towson State University, Towson, Maryland, she began her teaching career serving nine years as an elementary and middle school teacher.

After earning a M. Ed. in Reading from Towson State University, she spent seven years at the high school level in Troy, Alabama, as a developmental reading teacher. In this capacity she was successfully involved in numerous grant writing activities and literally transformed her developmental reading classroom into a state-of-the-art computer teaching lab as part of a dropout prevention project. Utilizing the Josten's WICAT Learning Lab, she was able to assist at-risk students with learning problems, and simultaneously the students earn Carnegie units toward graduation. In addition, during this period, she was an adjunct professor for the Troy State University School of Education teaching undergraduate and graduate courses in Educational Technology.

In the spring of 1999 she became an instructor for Barton College in Wilson, North Carolina teaching introductory technology courses in the Business Department. During this time she also served as a technology consultant for a local insurance business in eastern North Carolina.

In the fall of 2001 she took a position as a technology teacher trainer coordinating a half million dollar grant for Polk County Public Schools, Florida. In spring of 2003 she assumed a newly created resource teacher specialist position coordinating the alternative certification program. Her research spans several topics, including educational technology, Preparing Today's Teachers for Tomorrow's Schools, and grant writing.

The Castelli's are co-authors of the textbooks *__Exploring the Foundations of American Education__*, (2006), Sheepdog Publishing and *__Social Foundations of American Education__*, 2nd edition, (2000), Carolina Academic Press.

Index

academic freedom, 126
accommodate, 52
adapt, 19, 52
administrators, iii, v, viii, 25, 76,
  100, 101, 109, 127, 128, 137, 142,
  144, 145, 146, 147, 182, 211
analysis/synthesis, 56
appearance
  interview, 9, 211
application, 8, 11, 56
applications, 8, 11
  practical, 39, 69
  technology, 4
articles, 87, 193, 197
assimilate, 52
attendance, 23, 25, 84, 116, 120, 141,
  158
Bandura, Alberto, 55, 62
behavior, 26, 50, 55, 58, 59, 88, 89,
  90, 92, 93, 100, 101, 137, 143,
  162, 163, 174, 217
Bloom, Benjamin, 56, 62, 67
bodily-kinesthetic, 54
Brain-Based Learning, 57, 62
Campbell, Donald, 33
cassette recording, 162
certification, 127, 211
chaperones, 121
chart, 37, 40, 56, 71, 176
child abuse, 173
Child Benefit Theory, 130
civil disobedience, 126
classroom management, iii, 6, 83, 92,
  115, 177, 181, 211
Cognitive Development, 52
collaboration, 151, 186
collaborative, 53

colleagues, 85, 87, 93, 101, 103, 107,
  157, 160, 192, 197, 199, 201, 202,
  203
communication, 26, 58, 139, 176
community, 135, 151, 152, 194
comprehension, 56
concrete operations, 52
confront, 125
consequences, 25, 26, 51, 55, 58, 88,
  89
cooperative learning, 52, 53, 57, 68,
  82, 179
corporal punishment, 89, 116, 123,
  173
counsel, 125
creation
  creativity, v, 36, 56
creativity, 37, 39, 56, 76, 79, 86, 97,
  182
critical thinking, xiii, 65, 67, 82, 168
cross-examine, 125
curriculum, iii, xv, 27, 28, 47, 73, 74,
  75, 80, 126, 131, 152, 161, 162,
  167, 169, 196, 207
dangerous substance, 128, 129
database, 5, 23, 157
debate, 37, 56, 73, 119
diagram, 37
disciplinary hearing, 125
discussion, 37, 42, 50, 52, 53, 54, 69,
  70, 71, 119, 144, 163, 175, 176,
  182
diverse learners, 179
diversion, 104
documentation, 123, 139
due process, 125
DVD, 163
effectiveness, 122
Erikson, Eric, 51, 62

evaluation, 33, 35, 36, 37, 40, 43, 56, 67, 69, 212
evidence, 125, 211
exceptional children, 187
exercise, 2, 24, 102, 114
expectations, 6, 26, 33, 35, 58, 74, 86, 89, 92, 141, 143, 147, 162, 163, 183
expert, 199
exploration, 49, 54, 56, 99, 163, 182
extrinsic reinforcement, 58
fair, 35, 55, 88, 89, 147, 161, 181
feedback, 15, 40, 57, 63, 161
field trips, 75, 171
First Amendment, 118
focused attention, 57
formal operations, 52
fourteenth amendment, 127
Fourth Amendment, 125
fraternize, 131
games, 164
Gardner, Howard, 33, 37, 54, 62
gifted
    students, 182, 187, 188
Ginot, Haim, 191
government, 27, 118, 119
guest speakers, 21, 74, 87, 190
guidelines, 93, 123, 126, 130, 141, 143, 175
health, 102, 115
Hierarchy of Needs, 50
hobby, 106
hyperactive
    ADHD, 180
identity vs role confusion, 51
industry vs inferiority, 51
instruction, 27, 33, 34, 70, 82, 130, 145, 155, 179, 180, 217
    differentiated, 70
    direct, 69
interest, 80
interests, 57, 70, 86, 140
International Reading Association, 190
interpersonal, 54, 179
interpreter, 125

Interstate New Teacher Assessment and Support Consortium, 190
intrapersonal, 54
intrinsic reinforcement, 58
job search, 212
journals, xv, 81, 87, 161, 183, 187, 193, 196, 197, 198
K0 police dog, 128
kinesthetic, 54, 179
knowledge, 2, 7, 34, 49, 55, 56, 65, 66, 70, 103, 189
Kohlberg, Lawrence, 59, 62
Kohn, Alfie, 34
language development, 53
learning environment, 57, 58, 137
legal, 94, 116, 121, 123, 126, 142
Lemon Test, 119
lesson, 5, 28, 48, 54, 64, 67, 69, 82, 84, 85, 86, 120, 157, 180, 192, 200, 209
lesson plan book, 120
logical-mathematical, 54
magazines, 161, 193
malfeasance, 120
Maslow, Abraham, 50, 62
materials, 2, 19, 20, 21, 22, 27, 72, 74, 76, 84, 138, 147, 162, 163, 164, 183, 192, 197, 198, 201
medical records, 131
Mentally Retarded
    mild, mederate, 181
mentor, 31, 192
metal detectors, 129
minute of silence, 118
misbehaving. *See*
misfeasance, 120
model, 55, 76, 79, 98, 103, 163, 176, 192
moral development, 59
Moral Development, 62
motivation, xiii, 24, 65, 81, 83
multiple intelligences, 37, 54
musical, 37, 54, 83, 106, 179
national certification, 200
National Education Association, 32, 136, 153, 190, 206, 208
naturalist, 54

nonfeasance, 120
nonverbal, 58
nutrition, 102
organization, 19, 94, 99, 103, 122,
    145, 157, 190, 197
organize, 143, 157
ownership, 25
parent involvement, 153
Parent Teacher Organization, 194,
    201
parent/guardian, 23, 75, 94, 139, 140,
    142, 176
patience, 51, 109
peer tutoring, 55, 139, 179, 181, 182
peripheral perceptions, 57
philosophy of teaching, 5, 6
Piaget, Jean, 52, 62
PL 94-142, 172
plan, 22, 34, 52, 53, 67, 68, 70, 71,
    72, 74, 75, 76, 84, 90, 143, 151,
    156, 159, 162, 163, 171, 177
planning, xvii, 1, 17, 24, 34, 35, 67,
    73, 87, 109, 180, 192
politics, 51
portfolio, 3, 5, 10
positive reinforcement, 90
potential hazards, 131
praise, 5, 43, 55, 58, 69, 72, 117,
    146, 176
prayer, 118, 119
preoperations, 52
presentation, 73, 74, 87, 125, 160,
    196, 199, 219
principal, 88, 90, 93, 106, 126, 142,
    174, 175, 178, 200, 209
private, 122, 126, 130
private schools, 15, 130
problem-solving, 38, 39, 54, 57, 72,
    83
procedures, 58, 86, 101, 120, 143,
    146, 181
processing, 57, 123, 154
professional journals, 197
professionalism, xiii, 110, 189
project, 27, 48, 68, 73, 76, 159, 160,
    168, 177, 220
punctualtiy, 145

punishment, 58, 59, 121
    corporal, 173
rally around the flag, 119
record keeping, 23
referral, 175
relaxation, 107, 109, 115
religion, 51, 118, 119, 130
reprimands, 55
requirements, 127, 130, 131, 211
resume, 1, 3, 4, 5, 16, 142
rewards, 90
role model, 6, 53, 55, 103, 176, 192
routines, 25, 181
rules, 25, 26, 37, 51, 58, 72, 86, 89,
    92, 101, 125, 131, 137, 143, 146,
    156
rules and procedures, 143
safety, 94, 116, 120, 128, 131, 173,
    174
scaffolding, 51
schedule, 107, 131, 159
school district policy, 193
school law, xiii, 116, 134, 136, 219
search, 16, 32, 82, 85, 128, 159, 169,
    171
searches, 129
secular, 118, 119, 130
seizure, 128
sensiorimotor, 52
Skinner, B. F., 58, 63
Social Modeling
    Bandura, Alberto, 55
social transmission, 52
space, spatial, 41, 54
special services, 130
spoiled child, 172
spreadsheet, 5, 23, 139, 158
Stage Development, 51
standardized examinations, 130
strategies, v, 1, 41, 50, 51, 52, 53, 57,
    72, 73, 100, 115, 139, 179, 181
strengths, 42, 54, 68, 181, 209
stress management, iii, 113, 114,
    115, 219
student involvement, 73
student teachers, 31, 131, 135
subject matter, 84, 126, 162

substitute, 11, 28, 84, 120, 154
suicide, 174
support, 1, 2, 54, 93, 94, 99, 103,
 122, 137, 141, 143, 146, 175, 177,
 182, 183, 192, 194, 201, 203
taxonomies, 56
teacher shortage, 1
teachers handbook, 131
teacher's pet, 177
teaching methods, 87
technology, xv, 3, 66, 154, 156, 159,
 160, 161, 164, 171, 181, 182, 183,
 196, 199, 220
television, 65, 163, 201

tenure, 127
time management, 105
venn diagrams, 41, 72
video recording, 162
violence, 175
vocabulary development
 Vygotsky, Lev, 53
volunteer, 2, 7, 94, 122, 192, 194,
 199, 201
Vygotsky, Lev, 53
wait time, 51, 71, 73
weapon, 128, 129, 175
witness, 123, 128
word processing, 41, 156, 157

Alignment with Florida Educator Accomplished Practices

It is a reality that there is a tremendous teacher shortage in many states of the United States. Colleges of education cannot provide the great number of teachers that are needed, so it has become necessary to attract professionals from other graduating degrees and those who seek to change careers. Programs have been developed by various states and the school districts to provide the preparation that is needed to help these graduates and career changers to enter the classroom. Many enter the classroom with little preparation and school districts are working diligently to provide the support and funding to assist these teachers.

The career changers have become titled as alternative certification teachers because they have a degree other than education and are doing alternative routes to teaching. For many it means taking college courses again as outlined by the department of education in their state. Some are fortunate enough to find colleges that offer them education courses at the masters' level since these teachers are required to already have a minimum of a bachelor's degree. Many are taking part in professional development that is offered through the school districts. These programs are guided by state and federal guidelines as well as the No Child Left Behind Act.

After working with the Alternative Certification Program in Florida, we realized that our book could be a valuable resource for alternative certification teachers, those coming to education from other education degrees or career changes. Having our roots now in Florida, we have chosen the Florida Educator Accomplished Practices to align with the chapters of this book. However, other states with similar standards may find these very helpful.

On the next page is a table that provides the Florida Educator Accomplished Practices aligned with the chapters and pages of this book.

Florida Educator Accomplished Practice	Chapter	Pages
Assessment	3: Evaluation / Assessment	33-48
Communication	9: Working wth Parents and Administrators	43, 86, 101, 103, 137-153
Continuous Learning	1: Acquiring a Teaching Position; 7: Dealing With Stress; 12: Professionalism	1-16, 100-115, 189-208
Critical Thinking	5: Motivation and Critical Thinking	65-82
Diversity	11: Meeting the Needs of Diverse Students	173-188
Ethics	8: Know the Essentials of School Law	116-136
Human Development and Learning	4: Understanding Students and Your Subject	49-64
Knowledge of the Subject	4: Understanding Students and Your Subject	49-64
Learning Environments	6: Classroom Management	50, 55, 59, 68, 83-99
Planning	1: Acquiring a Teaching Position; 2: Starting the Year Off Right	1-16, 17-32, 84, 105
Role of the Teacher	12: Professionalism	110, 189-208
Technology	10: Utilizing Technology	154-172

"There's no word in the language I revere more than 'teacher.' My heart sings when a kid refers to me as his teacher, and it always has. I've honored myself and the entire family of man by becoming a teacher."

- Pat Conroy, Prince of Tides

"It is paradoxical that many educators and parents still differentiate between a time for learning and a time for play without seeing the vital connections between them."

- Leo Buscaglia, author, educator

"Most teachers have little control over school policy or curriculum or choice of texts or special placement of students, but most have a great deal of autonomy inside the classroom. To a degree shared by only a few other occupations, such as police work, public education rests precariously on the skill and virtue of the people at the bottom of the institutional pyramid."

- Tracy Kidder

"In a completely rational society, the best of us would be teachers and the rest of us would have to settle for something less."

- Lee Iacocca